DAVID JONES

Diversity in Unity

David Jones, *Aphrodite in Aulis*, 1941, Tate Gallery

DAVID JONES
Diversity in Unity

Studies of his Literary and Visual Art

edited by

BELINDA HUMFREY AND ANNE PRICE-OWEN

UNIVERSITY OF WALES PRESS
CARDIFF
2000

British Library Cataloguing-in-Publication Data.
A catalogue record for this book is available from the British Library.

ISBN 0-7083-1564-X

The publishers wish to acknowledge the financial assistance of Swansea Institute Research and Postgraduate Sub-committee towards the publication of this volume.

PR
6019
.053
Z482
2000

Typeset by Action Publishing Technology, Gloucester
Printed in Great Britain by Cambrian Printers, Aberystwyth

Contents

Illustrations

Notes on Contributors

A. M. (DONALD) ALLCHIN, honorary professor, University of Wales, Bangor, was previously canon of Canterbury Cathedral and director of the St Theosevia Centre for Christian Spirituality, Oxford. He has published mainly on the history of Christian spirituality, and on the frontiers between literature and religion, most recently concentrating on Wales; his latest books are *Praise Above All: Discovering the Welsh Tradition* (University of Wales Press, 1991) and *God's Presence Makes the World: The Celtic Vision through the Centuries in Wales* (Darton, Longman & Todd, 1996).

WILLIAM BLISSETT, professor emeritus of English, University College, University of Toronto, has published extensively on Edmund Spenser, Shakespeare, Ben Jonson and Literary Wagnerism. He was editor of the *University of Toronto Quarterly* (1965–76) and a co-editor of the *Spenser Encyclopedia* (University of Toronto Press, 1988). He first met David Jones in 1959, visited him frequently until his death in 1974, and published a memoir, *The Long Conversation* (Oxford University Press, 1981).

EWAN CLAYTON, calligrapher, was brought up near Ditchling, Sussex, home to the calligrapher Edward Johnston and to the Guild of Craftsmen founded by Eric Gill in which his mother and grandfather were weavers. For some years a Benedictine monk at Worth Abbey, he now divides his time between commissions and lecturing throughout Europe and North America. He is visiting lecturer at the Roehampton Institute for which he devised their current BA Calligraphy programme. In summer months he works as a consultant at the Palo Alto Research Centre of the Xerox Corporation, researching the uses of documents in contemporary workplaces.

THOMAS DILWORTH, professor of English, University of Windsor, Ontario, has published numerous articles on nineteenth- and twentieth-century authors, from Lear to Joyce and Virgil Thomson but principally on David Jones, in addition to four books including the monumental *The Shape of Meaning in the Poetry of David Jones* (University of Toronto Press, 1988). His *David Jones, a Life* is forthcoming from Jonathan Cape.

GERAINT EVANS, lecturer in Celtic and deputy director of the Language Centre, University of Sydney, has published *A Reader's Guide to Modern Welsh* (University of Sydney, 1993) and a range of articles on printing history, the latest in his co-edited *Origins and Revivals: Proceedings of the First Australian Conference of Celtic Studies* (Sydney, 1999). His edition of the correspondence between David Jones and Saunders Lewis, *The Whole Paludament of Welshness*, is forthcoming in 2000 from the Gregynog Press.

A. C. EVERATT, lecturer in Continuing Education, University of Newcastle-upon-Tyne, has published numerous articles on philosophy and some on history.

TOM GOLDPAUGH, assistant professor of English, Marist College, Poughkeepsie, New York, has published several articles on David Jones in periodicals including *The Journal of Modern Literature* (1994) and *Renaissance* (1999).

JEREMY HOOKER, poet, is a professor in the School of English and Creative Studies, Bath Spa University College, having taught previously at University of Wales, Aberystwyth, and the University of Groningen. He has published ten volumes of poetry starting with *Soliloquies of a Chalk Giant* (1974), most recently *Our Lady of Europe* (Enitharmon, 1997). His numerous critical works include studies of David Jones and John Cowper Powys and three books on literature of place: *Poetry of Place* (Carcanet, 1982); *The Presence of the Past* (Poetry Wales Press, 1987); and *Writers in a Landscape* (University of Wales Press, 1996).

BELINDA HUMFREY, formerly head of the Department of English, University of Wales, Lampeter, taught previously at the universities of Oxford and Reading. She has published widely on the creative process with focus on a dozen Welsh writers in English, from Henry Vaughan and John Dyer to Glyn Jones and R. S. Thomas, giving special attention to John Cowper Powys in books which include *Recollections of the Powys Brothers* (Peter Owen, 1980) and *John Cowper Powys's 'Wolf Solent': Critical Studies* (University of Wales Press, 1990). She was founding editor of *The New Welsh Review* (1988–91) and is editor of *The Powys Review* (1977 to the present).

ANNE PRICE-OWEN, senior lecturer in the Faculty of Art and Design, Swansea Institute of Higher Education, has published a range of articles on visual art, mainly Welsh and often in relation to poetry, notably on Brenda Chamberlain, Eric Gill, Gwen and Augustus John, Ray Howard-Jones, Christine Kinsey and R. S. Thomas, in *Planet, Poetry Wales* and *The New Welsh Review*. She relaunched the David Jones Society in 1996 and edits *The David Jones Journal*.

DEREK SHIEL, painter, sculptor, critic and practising psychotherapist, has published articles on David Jones, edited an *Agenda* edition of Jones's letters (1996) and is the co-author with Jonathan Miles of *David Jones: The Maker Unmade* (Seren Books, 1995).

R. S. THOMAS has been abundantly recognized throughout his lifetime as one of the few outstanding poets of the twentieth century and recently as worthy of the Nobel Prize for Literature (nomination 1996), an award which was then given to a lesser but politically fashionable poet. His score of volumes of brilliant lyrics on the spiritual condition of man from *Stones of the Field* (1946) to *No Truce with the Furies* (1995), with a *Collected Poems* (1993), is complemented by his prose writings such as found in his *Selected Prose* (Poetry Wales Press, 1983) and *R. S. Thomas, Autobiographies*, tr. J. W. Davies (Dent, 1997).

Acknowledgements

The editors wish to acknowledge their gratitude to the David Jones Estate for granting copyright clearance on the reproductions of all visual works by David Jones in this volume. They also wish to thank the following for kind permission to reproduce photographs and illustrations as follows:

David Jones, *Aphrodite in Aulis* (frontispiece) by permission of the Tate Gallery, London 1999.

David Jones, *Goat* (p. 28) by permission of Austin Desmond Fine Arts, London.

William Holman Hunt, *The Scapegoat* (p. 31) by permission of The Walker Art Gallery, Liverpool.

David Jones, Frontispiece to *In Parenthesis* (p. 34), David Jones, Tailpiece to *In Parenthesis* (p. 35), David Jones, *Petra im Rosenhag* (p. 98) by permission of the National Museums & Galleries of Wales.

Robert Rauschenberg, *Monogram* (p. 39) by permission of Moderna Museet Stockholm (The National Art Museums of Sweden).

David Jones, *Optima Goreu Musa* (p. 60), David Jones, *Cara Wallia Derelicta* (p. 61) by permission of the National Library of Wales.

David Jones, *Prudence Pelham* (p. 96) by permission of The Potteries Museum and Art Gallery, Stoke on Trent.

David Jones, *The Rime of the Ancient Mariner*, i–iv (p. 122), David Jones, *The Rime of the Ancient Mariner*, v–viii (p. 123) are reproduced by kind permission of Paul Hills.

David Jones, *The Artist* (front jacket), David Jones, *Dancing Bear* (p. 5), David Jones, *Elizabeth, Petra and Joanna Gill* (p. 93), David Jones, *Escaping Figure with Trinkets* (p. 95) from private collections by permission.

Abbreviations

A   *The Anathemata: Fragments of an Attempted Painting* (London: Faber, 1952)

DG   *The Dying Gaul* (London: Faber, 1978)

DGC   *Dai Greatcoat: A Self-Portrait of David Jones in his Letters* (London: Faber, 1980)

EA   *Epoch and Artist: Selected Writings* (London: Faber, 1959)

IP   *In Parenthesis* (London: Faber, 1937)

RQ   *The Roman Quarry and Other Sequences* (London: Agenda, 1981)

SL   *The Sleeping Lord and Other Fragments* (London: Faber, 1974)

Introduction

ANNE PRICE-OWEN

Diversity in unity is a fundamental and distinctive, if often over-looked, feature of the art of poet/painter David Jones (1895–1974), in both his visual and his literary work. It is a characteristic found in a diverse range of approaches to Jones's concepts of life and his techniques of artistic presentation.

The target of this collection of essays dealing with Jones's life and the broad range of his work is diversity in unity. Yet despite the variety of topics covered by the contributors, the essays themselves have much in common. Sometimes they refer to similar subject matter or incidents in Jones's life which affected his work and output. Each critic discusses these features from different perspectives relating to their chosen sphere of interest. Some essayists examine different themes, often in relation to the works of artists and writers not commonly associated with Jones. Some focus on Jones's literature, a number on his visual art, while others relate to both art forms. Nevertheless, all are unified by their investigation into much of the diverse and complex material which comprises Jones's literature and art. Inevitably, cross-referencing and overlapping occurs, although from divergent angles, according to the central issues of the authors concerned. Ultimately, through the integration of themes and the incorporation of common material, this collection is a synthesis of variegated parts where unity operates within the diversity, and vice versa. Overall, these articles represent an inter-disciplinary approach to Jones, whereby disparate strands and methods in Jones's work are reconciled and consolidated, demonstrating his predilection for perceiving the congruent in the incongruent within his quest for creative and spiritual integration. That being the case, the sum of the parts is greater than the whole.

The essays in this book are arranged to reflect the complexity, diversity and unity which typify so much of Jones's creative œuvre. Jeremy Hooker starts by opening a doorway for the fairly new reader while yet introducing novel perspectives for specialized readers of Jones. The initial discussion is of *In Parenthesis*, probably Jones's best-known text. Because Hooker covers Jones's works chronologically, as well as prose and poetry, together with informative biographical details, the article tackles Jones's quest for unity in his creativity from his sources and in his religious inclination.

The strong religious-philosophical impetus in Jones's search for unities in his work is a predominant subject of the earlier studies in this collection, although naturally it is a concern in later studies. Approaching Jones's originality within a line of nineteenth- and twentieth-century perceptions, William Blissett uses biblical quotations as well as a variety of visual images and First World War poets' writings which chart the scapegoat's curious history; he explores Jones's theme of the 'scapebeast', in addition to offering some interesting sidelights on the painter-poet's representations of the sacramentality of the world. The concept of the sacramental quality of life is central to Thomas Dilworth's study of the religious philosopher Jacques Maritain, and his profound influence on Jones. Ewan Clayton concentrates on Jones's union of drawing and painting as well as text and image, in his interpretation of Jones's painted inscriptions. In his comparative study of Jones and the Scottish philosopher, Alasdair MacIntyre, who followed the religious principles of Maritain also, A. C. Everatt finds the essential likenesses between the two scholars. This enquiry relates to the foregoing accounts, which focus variously on Jones as both writer and artist, thus supporting Everatt's claim that Jones is not a 'doer' but a 'maker'.

Religion is a bearer of tradition. One of Hooker's concerns is Jones's fusion of traditions and cultures. A concern with culture, ancient and new, may be seen as a major ingredient of the middle group of our studies. However, because their subject is the art of David Jones, all these studies inevitably slip also into considerations of the minute particulars, the minute cross-references and large out-references, and the playful and serious concentrations on and of visual and verbal text which characterize Jones's composition – and are the main focus of the later critical essays of this collection.

One of Jones's trademarks is perseverance, which A. M. Allchin discovers in his exploration of Jones's private letters, wherein Jones considers the tradition of Wales and the Welsh language. The matter of Wales and national identity is addressed by Geraint Evans with recourse to the poem 'The Sleeping Lord'. Jones's determination to revitalize the image of Wales in the twentieth century is apparent in this scrutiny of the poem's language and vocabularies. Language, both visual and verbal, is of significance to Anne Price-Owen who claims that, given his methodology, which is firmly fixed in the twentieth century, Jones demonstrates his sympathy for the feminists' cause. This is illustrated in both his visual and his literary texts, in which Price-Owen identifies feminist principles. Female qualities are also what Derek Shiel considers in his study of Jones's conflict between obeying religious doctrines and realizing his true vocation. This dilemma was manifested in Jones's two mental break-downs, one of which resulted in his giving up painting and denying his true nature. This insight into Jones's private life is balanced by Belinda Humfrey's essay, which examines some of the limitations brought by Jones's search for unity, by means of a critical analysis of his 1929 illustrations for Coleridge's *The Rime of the Ancient Mariner* in conjunction with his essay on the same subject of 1964. The interweaving of word and image discussed by Humfrey is considered again in a study of Jones's literary texts by Tom Goldpaugh. He explores Jones's manuscripts and experimental writings in a convincing argument which proposes that all of Jones's writing could be published as one literary work. This view is framed by R. S. Thomas's concluding essay where he elaborates on Jones's circular and labyrinthine forms. Although Thomas restricts himself to Jones's writings, the reader may draw parallels between what Thomas says of the poetry and does not say about Jones's visual art.

David Jones was born in Brockley, Kent, in 1895. His father, a Welsh printer's overseer, was from Flintshire, and his mother, although brought up in the Pool of London, was of Italian descent. His parents' mixed origins are of relevance when considering diversity in unity and David Jones. Although Jones made only a few visits to Wales, and lived there for barely four years from 1924 to 1928, he consciously identified with his father's people and the Welsh culture. Nevertheless, it was to his mother's country with its ancient Roman heritage that he looked for much of his inspiration and ideas also. He worked mainly in England and his works are sprinkled with allusions to English writers and artists. As Jeremy Hooker makes clear, Jones drew on all three cultures as sources of his artistic purposes, reconciling them through his unique and holistic vision to the extent that this amalgamation forms the subject of much of his literary and visual work.

His decision to become an artist also derives from his parents. His mother was a competent watercolourist and encouraged his artistic bent. Moreover, his father often brought home examples of his printing, and the young Jones took text and illustration for granted, a combination which led to his preoccupation with word and image. But, to start with, he attended Camberwell School of Art, and in 1914 completed his training with ambitions of becoming an illustrator of Welsh legends, or an animal painter. These may appear somewhat divergent interests but,

despite his initial plans being thwarted, Jones was to develop a vocabulary in both poetry and painting in which Welsh legends and animals are
significant.

The relationship between Jones's visual and verbal art extends beyond
these common themes. By 1930 he had earned a reputation as a painter
and an engraver/illustrator. Jones's interest in illustrating texts was
further realized by his decision to 'make a shape in words' (*IP*, x). His
subject matter, like that of the majority of his paintings, was related to
personal experience. He wrote about images and events he recalled from
serving in the First World War as a foot soldier on the Western Front.
His poem *In Parenthesis* (1937) contains many details about the soldier's
life in the trenches. His story does not dwell entirely on the personal and
contemporary, however, for war is a recurring activity of mankind. In
citing incidents peculiar to himself and his comrades, Jones invests them
with connotations relating to wars of the past, combining the wartime
duties of Roman soldiers with those of the warriors from *Y Gododdin*.
Such allusions, and by implication comparisons, ensure that 'It was from
the *particular* that he made the *general* shine out' (*DG*, 46). Hence, he
synthesized diverse strands which meet together to complete the whole.

Many of the themes in *In Parenthesis* are reiterated in Jones's visual
work. His illustrations for the poem's frontispiece and tailpiece are
obvious examples, as Blissett observes in his debate on the accuracy of
the nomenclature of scapegoat which is both soldier and ram. These
motifs recur in many other pictures. In order to comprehend these works
fully, we have to 'read' the pictures, decipher their common vocabularies and interpret them in the light of Jones's capacity for integrating
apparently disparate motifs.

Likewise, if we are to gain maximum comprehension of his poetry we
use the same methods. We absorb further knowledge when we consider
the layout of his text as if it were a picture; partly prose and partly
verse, Jones's writing is crammed with complex textures and techniques.
Some passages are lyrical, other sections are deliberately prosaic, so that
Jones conveys his meaning by means of rhythm and language. He also
makes much of typographical layout: sentences may be long and wieldy,
or short and succinct; lines and sentences are broken and divided by
spaces, sometimes before a line starts and often in mid-sentence. He
terminates lines abruptly; he enjoys using parentheses; he delights in
mixes of foreign words and phrases, and ambiguities are ever present.
His poetry abounds in internal rhyme schemes, pararhymes, assonance
and alliteration. These are among the reasons Tom Goldpaugh gives for
Jones's collective works not being published as he had originally
planned; they require a hypertext which was virtually impossible to

print, given publishing conditions of the time. Reproducing colour plates of Jones's paintings has also been a publisher's nightmare, owing to the delicacy of colour and the variety of tones which characterize many of them. In pictorial terms, Jones's line is an indication of his drawing technique. Sometimes the line is nervous and frail, at other times it is strong and dominant, variable in length and also in the patterns and textures delineated. Jones's pictures are comparable to his literary works also in that they employ repetition of motifs and shapes, and their inversions. His verbal ambiguities are the equivalents of multivalent 'signs' in his pictures. *Dancing Bear* (fig.1) is such an example, where the animal has a number of connotative meanings as discussed by Blissett and Shiel respectively. On the face of it, Jones is more conscious of the added value of spaces in his literature than in his late paintings. This may be because he continued to source copious notes in his poetry, whereas his

Fig. 1: David Jones, *Dancing Bear* (1903)

paintings rework many of his primary motifs to the extent that the familiar viewer might regard them as clichés.

Jones's mythological paintings of the 1940s are often densely populated, as *Aphrodite in Aulis* (1941) (frontispiece) shows. Price-Owen analyses this work in considering gender in Jones's literary style and themes. She suggests that Jones may be seen as a feminist thinker, and advances her argument by demonstrating that the figure of Aphrodite is really a metaphor for Christ, or Arthur. But Jones, being male, must be seen as a masculine artist and therefore reflects this dichotomy through his art. Hooker makes similar conclusions by claiming that Jones's use of *patria* (fatherland) is a reference to the 'motherland', in his discussion of the Arthurian legend.

Myth and legend are aspects of history which fascinated Jones. He viewed them not as fanciful stories of past civilizations, but as metaphors for underlying truths. Accordingly, he refers to the Christian story as the *mythus*. Jones was an Anglican by upbringing, but during the war he witnessed a celebration of the Mass in a derelict barn. The reverence and faith of the participants affected him deeply, and may have reminded him of an incident from his childhood. His mother had asked her Quaker doctor why Quakers have no sacraments. The doctor replied that 'the whole of life is a sacrament'. Interestingly, Blissett, Dilworth and Allchin all mention the significance of this episode, but from diverse perspectives relating to their specific investigations concerning diversity in unity. Blissett examines the statement in relation to contrasting ideas about scapegoats, while Dilworth takes a different angle. Using it as evidence for Jones's belief that art and everything else, including relationships, have metaphysical significance, Dilworth analyses the extent of the Catholic philosopher Jacques Maritain's influence on Jones. Allchin, on the other hand, discusses Jones's concept of sacrament in his study of Jones and his knowledge of Welsh, especially that found in religious texts.

Jones's interest in religion was compounded in 1921 when he met Eric Gill, the vanguard artist-craftsman of the Catholic Church. That same year Jones converted to Catholicism and joined Gill's arts and crafts community at Ditchling. From this time he made little distinction between the fine and applied arts, though unlike Gill he retained a sense of the independence of each. Fine art was what he later came to regard as 'extra-utile' (*DG*, 178) whereas he considered that craft was both 'utile' and 'extra-utile' (*DG*, 179). Craft combines function and beauty, as seen in Chartres Cathedral, while fine art is non-functional, as in painting. Jones speaks 'of a duality in man ... over the whole of man's existence, a mutual intermingling of the utile and the inutile has characterised his cultures' (*DG*, 179). Jones argues his own case for making unity out of diversity in respect of mankind's creations. And in his appreciation of Eric Gill, his friend and mentor, he declares that 'His great passion was to make a unity of all his activities' (*EA*, 298), a sentiment equally applicable to Jones himself.

Perhaps Jones's best examples of blending these dual concerns is found in his long illustrated poem *The Anathemata* (1952), where text and images unite to render the complete work. Nevertheless, the text may be read without any recourse to the illustrations, just as these can be appreciated without reading the text. In fact, Jones made some of the illustrations before conceiving the completed poem, while others were specifically designed for it. A number of these are painted inscriptions which, being composed of fragments of texts using biblical, Anglo-Saxon, Welsh or occasionally English sources, reflect the overall character of *The Anathemata* which is subtitled 'fragments of an attempted writing'. Given the number of allusions Jones makes to his paintings in the poem, it could be argued that 'fragments of an attempted painting' would be an equally appropriate subtitle!

Perhaps the apotheosis of the union of word and image is to be found in Jones's painted inscriptions. In these, both art forms are interdependent, yet may be appreciated independently. Jones's alphabetical forms, where each is imbued with cultural pertinence depending on the origins of the language and textual sources, are unique, individual entities. When combined together in the lettered inscriptions, the words may be considered as ritualistic invocations.

This at least is the view of the calligrapher Ewan Clayton who reviews these works from a meditative perspective; they are familiar and also relay a physical presence. This presence is ascribed to the surfaces of artefacts which are adorned by inscriptions, namely tombs bearing hieroglyphics and epigraphs on tombstones. Often the word is not merely a means of recording, but is transformed into the memorial itself, rather like Jones's poetry, which is a recalling of something loved. He believed that words are incarnational: 'the Word is made stone' (*A*, 93), and stone is a metaphor for both Christ and Mary, as Price-Owen observes in her analysis of role reversals in Jones's art.

To Jones all art is 'incarnational': he believed 'that a work [of art] is a "thing" and not (necessarily) the impression of some other thing' (*EA*, 172). He compared this hypothesis with the doctrine of the Incarnation in declaring that

> what matters ... is whether or no the forms he [the artist] makes resolve
> themselves in such a way as to show forth, re-present, embody or make

> corporeal the incorporeal reality envisaged in the eye of his mind . . . its
> products are of the body . . . a sort of 'word made flesh'. (*DG*, 168)

He believed that all living things were endowed with both matter and
spirit which accounted for '"the unity of all made things"' (*EA*, 171).
These apparently incompatible features are addressed by Derek Shiel in
respect of the Church's teachings and their adverse effect on Jones's
visual art when he suffered his first mental breakdown in 1932.

The conflict in Jones's mind was compounded by his being surrounded
by Catholic friends (notably Eric Gill), who found fulfilment for their
emotional, sexual and intellectual needs, even to the point of rationaliz-
ing their behaviour. Several factors militated against Jones in his search
for similar fulfilment. Firstly, he had served in a war which entailed
widespread killing of his fellow men. In spite of the war's devastating
effects on Jones, it is clear from his letters that he enjoyed the cama-
raderie of the soldiers. His war period was one of the few episodes in
his adult life when he must have felt part of a family. His second
'family' period occurred when he settled in the Ditchling community,
which culminated in his engagement to Petra Gill in 1924. When he
joined the Gills on their move to Capel-y-ffin this life continued, apart
from his extended visits to Caldey Island. But in 1927 his engagement
was broken off. Jones devoted himself to his work, perhaps aware that
he did not have the means to support a family. In addition, his dedication
to art would seem to preclude any other relationships; he could not serve
two masters. Hence, his most productive period in the visual arts
commenced. However, from this time onwards he became a nomad,
staying with various friends for weeks, sometimes months, at a time.

The instability and upheaval of his life was countered by his accep-
tance of Maritain's philosophies which, as Dilworth shows, remained a
prevailing influence throughout his life. However, according to Shiel,
Jones's crisis of personal identity was exacerbated by his desire to follow
the Church's doctrine as well as art. Shiel and Dilworth respond differently to Jones's precept that 'the workman must be dead to himself while
engaged upon the work' (*A*, 12). Dilworth interprets the maxim as a
means of curtailing subjective emotions in the artwork, purporting that
this is the essence of artistic integrity. Conversely, Shiel intimates an
impending identity crisis by claiming that Jones was denying part of his
true self by adhering to his dictum.

In this collection of studies, the question of Jones and identity is
treated from several viewpoints, all of which demonstrate the complexities attributed to the whole man. Allchin and Geraint Evans
contextualize Jones's connections with Wales. Allchin focuses on the

question of the Welsh language, while the latter examines Jones's determination to revitalize the image of Wales in the twentieth century. Hooker disagrees with Evans in arguing that Rome, Wales and England are equally significant to Jones in respect of both language and culture. In discovering Jones's similarities with the philosopher MacIntyre, as both writers contemplate a twentieth-century world which has lost traditional identity, A. C. Everatt offers an alternative opinion, claiming that Jones is not a 'doer' but a 'maker' and that what he makes are stories.

'It was a dark and stormy night, we sat by the calcined wall; it was said to the tale-teller, tell us a tale, and the tale ran thus: it was a dark and stormy night . . .' This epigraph to *The Anathemata*, Jones's argosy of the Redeemer, sets the scene for the tale. Like its epigraph, the story's structure is circular. R. S. Thomas follows a similar circular line, albeit with labyrinthine ramifications, to which he alludes in his poem at the start of his essay. The poem acts as a preface to his meditations on the epigraph. Although Thomas claims that his 'is not a tidy presentation', it is a supremely tailored piece of writing. In any investigation of Jones's themes tidiness is hardly a paramount concern. Jones's writing is characterized by themes which digress, details which are tangential and layers of ancillary sub-themes, all of which strengthen, rather than detract from, the main argument.

The tale Thomas tells is analogous to Jones's, exploring time past and time present through evolutionary, mythopoeic and religious channels, ending where it begins, with the Mass. Thomas finishes his account similarly, with an invitation to come unto the Spirit, a sentiment with which Clayton concurs, seeing the journey as 'a dance with the line'. These are statements to which Jones would have consented, judging by his allegory: 'Now making a work is not thinking thoughts but accomplishing a journey' (*A*, 33).

The journey Belinda Humfrey surveys is that of *The Ancient Mariner*, Jones's exploration in line engravings and an essay, concerned with an earlier poet's visual narrative of a voyage through spiritual crises to some sort of resolution. Jones's illustrations, by their omissions and readings, show more of his obsessions than Coleridge's.

Like Humfrey, Goldpaugh researches Jones's original, rather than edited, published versions. His essay deals with Jones's entire body of literature. Goldpaugh's findings suggest that all of this may be read as one long poem, where themes recur, intertwine and reappear with expanded meanings, so that they accrue in value. Given the validity of his discovery, one can credit Jones with meticulous literary solidarity, thus emphasizing his concern for unity in diversity. Indeed, Evans maintains that 'The Sleeping Lord' is a 'seamless' piece of writing, which suggests that Jones's attention to coherence is integral to his methods. The same may be said of Jones's visual work. A portrait, a still life, a narrative scene or an inscription may stand as a work in its own right without consulting other visual material. When these are investigated collectively, they chart Jones's development as an artist who was intent on fusing the two disciplines with which he engaged: painting and poetry.

Goldpaugh's survey of the manuscripts comprising what we know as *The Roman Quarry* shows that this section of the work exhibits Jones's shift from an essentially linear, temporal sequence to a spatial structure, such as is found in *The Anathemata*. The additional insertions and amendments to the manuscripts also show how the structure of the work moves from a linear narrative to an inward and downward direction, establishing the labyrinthine text. In one of his most convincing conclusions Goldpaugh argues that 'The Tutelar of the Place' is at the centre of the narrative script, just as 'The Lady of the Pool' is pivotal to *The Anathemata*. Both female characters are enclosed in a 'temenos', a sacred place. But as Clayton and Price-Owen also observe, Jones plays with lines and boundaries. They can simultaneously protect and imprison, which produces further tension in the poems while also extending the metaphor of the labyrinth. Goldpaugh maintains that Jones's intention was to construct a work which was a protective labyrinth, one which would literally enclose the endangered signs of our culture.

Finally, we can claim that the work of art is itself a temenos, and therefore a valid sign for reporting on the past while being comprehensible in the present. Such speculations imply that all of Jones's writing could be rearranged and published as one long labyrinthine poem, where characters are integrated into the fabric of the recurring motifs and themes. This equates with Jones's approach to his visual work. He was loath to sell, or part with, many of his pictures because for him they possessed an accumulative value whereby they enlightened and enhanced one another. His attitude is quoted by Allchin: 'the artist's best . . . motto is found in . . . Psalm CXXII . . . about Jerusalem being builded as a city whose parts are united in one.' This indicates that Jones's entire work constitutes one unified whole, which was governed by his desire to emulate Nennius whom he quotes at the outset of the Preface to *The Anathemata*: '"I have made a heap of all that I could find."' Jones's endeavours in both his poetic and his visual works show that through diverse explorations he completed his task and created a unity out of that diversity.

David Jones and the Matter of Wales

JEREMY HOOKER

'From about the age of six', David Jones said, 'I felt I belonged to my father's people and their land' (*DG*, 23). His father, James Jones, who was born in 1860 in north Wales, came from a family that was 'Welsh-speaking on both sides' (*EA*, 25). James Jones was, however – in his son's words – 'of that generation . . . whose parents were determined that he should be as English as possible' (*DG*, 31), and therefore discouraged him from using the Welsh language. What happened subsequently is, in outline, a familiar story of the period. James Jones left Wales to work in London; he continued to feel Welsh, but he lacked a grasp of the Welsh-language tradition. He married an English woman from a Thames-side family who had 'an Italian strain on her maternal side' (*DG*, 21). Their son, as he grew up, developed an acute imaginative awareness of his mixed heritage – Welsh, English, Latin. He felt that he had been deprived of his father's *patria*.

Since Jones lived most of his life in London, it is easy to underestimate the importance of his actual contacts with the land of his fathers. He was conditioned by his experience as a private with the Royal Welch Fusiliers on the Western Front from 1915 to 1918, which gave him the companionship of Welshmen. He spent one of the most emotionally intense and intellectually fertile periods of his life living with Eric Gill and his family at Capel-y-ffin in the Black Mountains in 1925–6. He was then on the verge of his period of greatest creative activity, from 1928 to 1932, which was foreshadowed by paintings in which he responded to 'the strong hill-rhythms and the bright counter-rhythms of the *afonydd dyfroedd*' (*EA*, 30). As a boy, his visits to relatives in north Wales had shown him 'visible and tangible survivals from a Welsh past in an, as yet, virtually unspoiled landscape' (*EA*, 27). He had identified his grandfather and his place with Welsh literary and mythological figures. Now, his stay at Capel-y-ffin enhanced his sense of the land of Wales, and his identification of it with native myth – the Arthurian cycle – that would first surface in *In Parenthesis*, which he began to write in 1928.

Jones's imagination fed on his *hiraeth* for Wales – for the Wales of his grandparents, which they had withheld from their son, and for a Wales made in a far older image, as part of Catholic Europe. It is true that he had a passion for the past, especially for the Wales that he believed to have 'gone under' in 1282, with the death of the last prince of independent Wales, Llywelyn ap Gruffudd, but it is not the whole truth. It is certainly far from true to say, as René Hague did, that 'it was the mother who won in determining the character of David's writing', and 'he was cut off from a Wales for which he had no more than a sentimental love' (*DGC*, 23). Jones was intensely concerned for the fate of the Welsh language and culture in the twentieth century, a concern which he shared with Welsh friends who were active in nationalist politics. His friendship with Saunders Lewis is particularly important in this context. The connection between their thinking about Wales in relation to the Catholic West makes it less easy to dismiss Jones's idea of Wales as a romantic dream. It is interesting to note that Saunders Lewis considered his friend to be an English poet.[1] From a different point of view, Jones's preoccupations illuminate the complex situation of the modern Anglo-Welsh writer, a situation brought about by the social and economic pressures behind Anglicization in his father's generation. T. S. Eliot provided yet another perspective when he described Jones as 'decidedly a Briton'.[2] The fuss over nomenclature may seem like academic trifling, but it is not. It indicates, rather, that Jones's writing and thinking go to the heart of issues concerning not only national identity in twentieth-century Britain, but also human identity in the modern world. For Jones, the human image, the image of man the artist, made by God in his likeness, was involved in the matter of Wales. This is why he says of Lance-Corporal Aneirin Merddyn Lewis, in *In Parenthesis*, he 'had somewhere in his Welsh depths a remembrance of the nature of man' (1–2).

> What makes the Arthurian thing important to the Welsh is that there is no other tradition at all equally the common property of all the inhabitants of Britain (at all events of those south of the Antonine Wall), and the Welsh, however separatist by historical, racial and geographical accidents, are devoted to the unity of this island. (*EA*, 216)

Jones's words from 'The Myth of Arthur' apply to what he intends to show in *In Parenthesis*. His book about the war on the Western Front from December 1915 to July 1916 is also about 'the unity of this island'. Jones's companions in the Royal Welch Fusiliers 'were mostly Londoners with an admixture of Welshmen'. Together the Londoners and the Welshmen 'bore in their bodies the genuine tradition of the Island of Britain'. Jones sees 'the Celtic cycle' underlying this tradition: 'a subterranean influence as a deep water troubling, under every tump in this Island, like Merlin complaining under his big rock' (*IP*, x–xi). His sources for it in *In Parenthesis* include Malory, the *Mabinogion* and the racial memory of his Welsh soldiers, especially Aneirin Lewis and Dai.

The 'texts' from *Y Gododdin* which Jones uses at the head of each part of *In Parenthesis* recall the 300 Welsh who fell in their attack on the English at Catraeth in the sixth century. The choice of these fragments, he says, 'connects us with a very ancient unity and mingling of races; with the Island as a corporate inheritance, with the remembrance of Rome as a European unity. The drunken 300 at Catraeth fell as representatives of the Island of Britain' (*IP*, 191–2). The sense of connection was vitally important to Jones. His concern for the past was not an antiquarian interest. He was a modernist, whose closest affinities were with Gerard Manley Hopkins, and who owed a stylistic debt to *The Waste Land* in *In Parenthesis*, and to *Finnegans Wake* in *The Anathemata*. At the same time, he was a writer of great originality who invented and extended modernist techniques. But Jones was also in intention a poet in the tradition of Aneirin, the early Welsh poet to whom the composition of *Y Gododdin* is ascribed. Jones too was, as he said of Aneirin, 'concerned with a recalling and appraisement of the heroes' (*EA*, 57–8). Like Aneirin, he commemorates the fallen companions and gains a kind of victory from the celebration of heroic defeat. He too appraises 'the men of valour'.

In Parenthesis is a poem in praise of heroes. Its heroism is not that of a Grenfell or a Brooke, which the disillusioned war poets invalidated, although it is also true to say that Jones's perspective is not Owen's or Sassoon's, either. He celebrates the courage of endurance, of goodness and kindness in adversity, of men who 'would make order, for however brief a time, and in whatever wilderness' (*IP*, 22). He does not glorify war. The 'texts' from *Y Gododdin* connect the men to the Celtic tradition of defeat. The allusions to the Battle of Camlann mark their contest as a betrayal, and an 'undoing of all things'. The poet says of both armies, however, the British and the German, 'They're worthy of an intelligent song for all the stupidity of their contest' (88–9). And they get it, for *In Parenthesis* is a celebration of humanity. Through these particular men, it shows the kind of being man is – a creature 'a little lower than the angels', a maker whose 'inventions are according to right reason even if you don't approve the end to which they proceed' (154).

The poem is rich in individual character. The differences among the

Welsh are accordingly as marked as the differences between the Welsh
and the English, and among the English. For example, we hear of
'nonconforming Captain Gwyn' who is 'stuffy about the trebled whisky
chits' (107), and – a sketch that would have delighted Caradoc Evans –
Quartermaster-Sergeant Hughes who had 'learned a trick by water / at
Pugh's Hygienic Dairy to the impoverishment of the Lord's people'
(73). Nor is it only men that the poem recalls. The epigraph to the book
is Aneirin's 'seinnyessit e gledyf ym penn mameu' ('His sword rang in
mother's heads'). Women's suffering is a fact of war that *In Parenthesis*
shows, as well as the men's longing for women, and especially for the
mother's protective embrace.

Homelands and Front, mothers and sons, are sometimes brought
together, as in the following passage:

> and where the Mother of Rivers bares her smooth bulk, where
> the little hills skip to wasted Gwaelod – where Sabrina rises:
> their Rachels weeping by a whitened porch
> and for the young men
> and for Dai and for Einon
> and for Jac Pryse, Jac Pryse plasterer's son. (131)

The *patria*, then, is also a motherland, in its women, and in its landscape and myths. In this connection I would like to recall what I think is
the most suggestive short piece ever written about Jones. In his introduction to the radio broadcast of 'The Dream of Private Clitus', Saunders
Lewis said: 'private soldier and Mother Earth belong to each other with
an intimacy that not even the shepherd can know. He befouls her, he
digs her, he sleeps on her, he lies on her in action and inaction,
wounded and unwounded, alive, dying and dead. She is Matrona,
Modron, Tellus, the Mother . . .'[3] Lewis proceeds to quote part of the
following invocation to her from the battle scene in *In Parenthesis*:

> – down on hands on hands down and flattened belly
> and face pressed and curroodle mother earth
> she's kind:
> Pray her hide you in her deeps
> she's only refuge against
> the ferocious pursuer
> terribly questing.
> Maiden of the digged places
>   let our cry come unto thee.
> *Mam*, moder, mother of me
> Mother of Christ under the tree

> reduce our dimensional vulnerability to the minimum –
> cover the spines of us
> let us creep back dark-bellied where he can't see
> don't let it.
> There, there, it can't, won't hurt – nothing
> shall harm my beautiful. (176–7)

Fear releases the most primitive instincts in the soldier; he is both a child who in his extremity cries out to his mother and imagines her words of comfort, and supplicant to primeval Mother Earth in the form of 'Mother of Christ' for her protection.

In my view, Lewis's comments go to the heart of the matter, in so far as it concerns Jones's feeling for the earth and the land. The feeling for the earth as womb in his writings is connected to his feeling for the land of Wales as a sacred enclosure. What was initially, perhaps, a visceral feeling of primary attachment, identified with his relation to his mother, was also integral to his religious experience, for which he found expression in myth. In his discussions of Arthur, Jones occasionally hints that, as Mars was originally a god of agriculture, so in some distant time lost in obscurity, Arthur was a goddess.[4] Explicitly in his prose, and with charged significance in his poetic imagery, he recalls 'the tradition of matriarchy, a thing of pre-Celtic provenance, working up through the Aryan patriarchy' (*EA*, 48). The comment of the Lady of the Pool in *The Anathemata*, 'What's under works up' (*A*, 164), is a locus of deep meaning in Jones's writings, and has a special relevance to what the Lady calls 'this Matriarch's Isle' (*A*, 145). The pagan myth connecting mankind and Mother Earth, who is 'both womb and grave' (*DG*, 142), pervades the writings. It is to be understood, of course, as everything in his work is, in the context of his Catholicism. As he wrote in a letter to René and Joan Hague, 'I suppose all my stuff has on the whole been central round the Queen of Heaven and cult hero – son and spouse' (*DGC*, 227). Behind this paper on Jones and the matter of Wales lies a desire to suggest the connections between 'matter', *materia poetica*, 'matrix' and 'mother', as they affect and are manifested in his work, and to show how the weave of etymologies coheres with the idea of Wales as the fatherland.

The principal Welsh figures in *In Parenthesis* are Aneirin Merddyn Lewis and Dai of the famous boast. The names of the former indicate his character as a rememberer, like the poet Aneirin, and his inheritance from the magician. Memory and magic are the chief qualities that Jones associates with the Welsh. Memory preserves the deep things of the past, which represent the 'ancient unity and mingling of races' in the

Island of Britain. Magic, as in the *Mabinogion*, is an imaginative and almost supernatural power, that belongs to man as 'a "borderer" . . . the sole inhabitant of a tract of country where matter marches with spirit' (*EA*, 86). In the Preface, Jones describes 'the Waste Land' of the Western Front as 'a place of enchantment'. Both the baleful enchantment of Welsh myth and its more spiritual transformations are present in the land under a curse.

Aneirin is contrasted with Watcyn, who 'knew everything about the Neath fifteen, and could sing *Sospan Fach* to make the traverse ring, [but] might have been an Englishman when it came to matters near to Aneirin's heart' (89). These are Welsh matters, and therefore matters of Britain, which include the legend that Aeneas's grandson, Brute, founded the British kingdom – a legend that connects the Island to Virgil and Homer and the prehistory of the West. Like Jones, Aneirin recalls Llywelyn 'ein llyw olaf', killed in December 1282; for Jones, a type of Christ, like Arthur, a Lord of the Christian order that connected the Romano-Welsh and their descendants to the remote beginnings of a human culture on the Island. Aneirin Lewis, then, is 'decidedly a Briton'. His death calls forth a moving elegy:

> No one to care there for Aneirin Lewis spilled there
> who worshipped his ancestors like a Chink
> who sleeps in Arthur's lap
> who saw Olwen-trefoils some moonlighted night
> on precarious slats at Festubert,
> on narrow foothold on le Plantin marsh –
> more shaved he is to the bare bone than
> Yspaddadan Penkawr. (155)

No one to care for him *there*, in the chaos of battle that unmakes all human order. Yet he is cared for, by the poet who, like Aneirin's name-sake, commemorates this man of valour, and by the Queen of the Woods who 'carries to Aneirin-in-the nullah a rowan sprig, for the glory of Guenedota'. She too is a figure who appraises in the spirit of the ancient Welsh poet: 'She knows what's due to this elect society' (185).

Dai's boast fulfils a similar function in the poem to that of Aneirin Lewis. In the broad terms of the Preface to *The Anathemata*, both figures 'call up . . . a whole world of content belonging in a special sense to the mythus of a particular culture and of concepts and realities belonging to mankind as such' (23–4). They represent the artist's abhorrence of 'any loppings off of meaning or emptying out, any lessening of the totality of connotation, any loss of recession and thickness through' (24). They fulfil the artist's role of delivering 'what has been delivered' to them, from the deposits. In the words of Stanley Spencer, which were to Jones the most succinct expression of the artist's business, they gather all in.[5] Specifically, what they deliver, what they gather in, are the things of the Island, things which constitute its unity – a unity that David Jones was well aware had been fractured after 1282, and was further broken up under the Tudors, but that remains, he believed, in the keeping of the Welsh. 'O Land! – O Bran lie under', exclaims Dai, invoking the protective power over the land invested in the Welsh myth. In the Preface to *In Parenthesis*, Jones says that 'Every man's speech and habit of mind were a perpetual showing' of the cultural unities of the Island. Aneirin Lewis and Dai, who 'articulates his English with an alien care', show in their speech and habits of mind things belonging to the Welsh mythus, and to history and legend, that represent the unity of the Island. Dai begins his boast, which Jones modelled not only on that of Taliesin but to recall 'Before Abraham was, I am', like a man with a long and fabulous tale to tell:

> My fathers were with the Black Prinse of Wales
> at the passion of
> the blind Bohemian king.
> They served in these fields,
> it is in the histories that you can read it, Corporal – boys
> Gower, they were – it is writ down – yes. (79)

And an English voice interjects, 'Wot about Methuselum, Taffy?' Humour is one of the soldier's most effective weapons of self-protection. Also, without a saving scepticism, Dai's sense of the presence of the past – and his author's – would be unbelievable.

In form and in content, in its marriage of form and content, the Latin inscription that faces the opening of *The Anathemata* embodies in minia-ture the whole of Jones's commemorative intention. In English translation it reads: 'To my parents and their forebears and to all the native people of the bright island of Britain'. The native elements Jones recalls in *The Anathemata* are German, Latin and Celtic. 'Together these three elements compose "the West": we are Germans, Latins, Celts and can apprehend only in a Latin, German and Celtic fashion' (*A*, 241). The native and indeed racial constituents of Jones's thinking would repay a detailed examination. Whatever the limitations of his idea of blood and soil, however, it must be realized that his vision both validates all cultures and is of a universal redemption. Thus, the Priest of the Household in 'The Sleeping Lord' recalls, at Mass,

the departed
of the entire universal orbis
from the unknown beginnings
unguessed millenniums back
until now. (*SL*, 86)

This accords with the belief expressed in a note to *The Anathemata* that
the Mass is offered on behalf 'of the whole argosy of mankind, and, in
some sense, of all sentient beings, and perhaps, of insentient too' (106).

It is in the particular, though, that Jones illumines the universal.
Again, in *The Anathemata*, Wales and the Welsh stand for 'the Island as
a corporate inheritance, with the remembrance of Rome as a European
unity'. In the words of 'Rite and Fore-Time':

Combroges bore us:
tottering, experienced, crux-signed
old Roma
the yet efficient mid-wife of us. (71–2)

In Parenthesis foreshadows the identification that is accomplished in
The Anathemata and 'The Sleeping Lord' between the land of Wales and
the Welsh tradition, or matter, embodied in religion, language, poetry,
history and myth. This may be seen, for example, in the following
passage about Snowdon:

Before the Irish sea-borne sheet lay tattered on the gestatorial
couch of Camber the eponym
            lifted to every extremity of the sky
by pre-Cambrian oreos-heavers
            for him to dream
the Combroges' epode.
In his high *sêt* there.
            Higher than any of 'em
south of the Antonine limits.
Above the sealed hypogéum
            where the contest was
and the great *mundus* of sepulture (there the *ver-tigérnus* was)
here lie dragons and old Pendragons
                    very bleached.
His unconforming bed, as yet
                    is by the muses kept.

And shall be, so these Welshmen say, till the thick
rotundities give . . . (67–8)

The temporal perspective is geological, or rather the context is the presence of the past, from before the ice lay over the pre-Cambrian mountains, on the couch of Camber, Aeneas's great-grandson who, in the legend, gave his name to Cambria. The summit of Snowdon is described as 'his high *sêt*', a Welsh word meaning seat or pew, that recalls the Nonconformist chapel. The image of 'the great *mundus* of sepulture (there the *ver-tigérnus* was)' invokes 'Moel yr Wyddfa', the Hill of the Burial Mound, and the 'traditions of imprisoned dragons and buried heroes' (68) associated with the peak of Snowdon. The tribute to the Nonconformist contribution to Welsh identity and its preservation is reinforced by the image of 'His unconforming bed', which conflates a geological and a religious term. This bed 'is by the muses kept'. The image thus brings together poetry and religion as powers that maintain the Welsh tradition. The whole passage is, in fact, a Welsh boast, as is further revealed by the allusion to the words of the old Welshman of Pencader to Henry II, recorded by Giraldus Cambrensis: 'Nor do I think, that any other nation than this of Wales, or any other language, whatever may hereafter come to pass, shall in the day of severe examination before the Supreme Judge, answer for this corner of the earth.'[6]

The effect of this and similar passages from *The Anathemata* and Jones's later writings may be compared to the Welsh philosopher J. R. Jones's idea of *cydymdreiddiad*, which Ned Thomas describes as 'that subtle knot of interpenetration, which ... grows in time (in people's consciousness) between a territory and its people and their language, creating a sense of belonging to a particular stretch of the earth's surface.'[7] It will be necessary for me later to qualify this comparison. Here I will add that in Jones's apprehension of things, in his embodied vision, language, poetry and religion are part of the very land of Wales. Hence the centrality of Arthur to his structure of ideas. Arthur, as one of the Celtic 'armed sleepers under the mounds', is associated with the landscape of the Forward Zone in *In Parenthesis*; he is also a type of Christ, 'the Protector of the Land, the Leader, the Saviour, the Lord of Order carrying a raid into the place of Chaos' (*IP*, 201). In Jones's late writing, the questioning form of 'The Sleeping Lord' projects his identification with both 'the first of the sleepers of / Pritenia' (*SL*, 71) and the land of Wales itself, which therefore represents the hope of restoring the Christian culture of the West, established from the foundation of the world.

The boast of 'the boatswain, from Milford', mediated by the Lady of the Pool, plays a similar role in *The Anathemata* to that of Dai in *In Parenthesis*. He too had much to tell of the legendary history and myth of the Island, of 'the fathering tars of old mother Troas', and Julius

Caesar, and 'the Saving Barque that Noë was master of'. He averred 'that his Maddoxes, Owenses, Griffins, and Company was a type of sea-king' (*A*, 150) and voyaged to America. He swore by many fabulous figures, and figures of doubtful historicity. He swore by the 'broidered tales' of Geoffrey of Monmouth, 'now deemed the most incontinent liar on record' (*A*, 152). So says the Lady of the Pool, but her scepticism, which salts the boatswain's extravagance with humour, also extends to the scepticism of the learned, who impugn fable. Her function at this point, therefore, is to make the matter of the boatswain's boast credible, in the spirit of a note on Troy Novant. This is worth quoting at length, since it is central to Jones's matter and his way of thinking about it. He says that in Caesar's *civitas Trinobantum*

> we have the origin of the legendary city of Trinovantum, or Troy Novant, which the work of Geoffrey of Monmouth made an integral part of our national mythological deposit, whereby, through the Trojan, Brute, of the line of Aeneas, Venus and Jove, our tradition is linked with all that that succession can be made to signify; and seeing what we owe to all that, the myth proposes for our acceptance a truth more real than the historic facts alone discover. (*A*, 124)

Hence the importance of *Historia Regum Britanniae* for Jones: Geoffrey's 'lies' in his pseudo-history preserve the connection that binds Britain to the religious and cultural heritage of the Mediterranean world. It is partly through Geoffrey that Britons are Europeans.

Jones's great boasters, Dai and the 'Welshook Milford bo's'n', make rich recallings of the things of the Island. In this, they are the opposite of another of his great monologists. This is the Tribune, the fact-man who has suppressed his love of his own home place in order to serve the Roman world-plan.

> Old rhyme, no doubt, makes beautiful
> the older fantasies
> but leave the stuff
> to the men in skirts
> who beat the bounds
> of small localities
> all that's done with
> for the likes of us
> in *Urbs*, throughout *orbis*. (*SL*, 50)

The apologist for empire has a word for all who, like Dai, and the boatswain, the Lady of the Pool, and the Tutelar of the Place, love 'place, time, demarcation, hearth, kin, enclosure, site, differentiated cult' (*SL*, 59). The word is 'fantasies'. The apologist rationalizes the severing of attachments to the past: 'Only the neurotic look to their beginnings' (*SL*, 51).

One answer to that allegation is, 'What's under works up.' The Lady of the Pool avers that if the 'sleepers' under the soil of London, Bran the Blessed and 'other hidden guardians and strength-givers', should 'stir, then would our Engle-raum in this Brut's Albion be like to come to some confusion' (*A*, 164). 'Engle-raum', of course, recalls *lebensraum*, and has a particular sting in the context of the city that was being blitzed during the period that Jones was working on *The Anathemata*. *Raum* is a word that needs glossing from his prose, before it can be shown in what sense the confusing of 'Engle-raum', in 'Brut's Albion' is an intention of his writings.

In 'Art in Relation to War' he speaks of the human species's 'rightful *imperium*, its native *Raum*, its double homeland along all the frontiers and uncertain borders of matter and spirit. Man, like King Hurlame, is Lord of the Two Marches, and must keep the difficult dignity of his dual role' (*DG*, 165). In 'Art and Democracy' the same idea calls up the same image: 'man is a "borderer", he is the sole inhabitant of a tract of country where matter marches with spirit' (*EA*, 86). The idea is cast in a militant form when, at the end of 'The Myth of Arthur', he recalls *Dewi Sant*,

> within his wattles at Mynyw among the Irish-Welsh of the extremity of what is now Pembrokeshire, training his shock-troops in the technics of an offensive which had for its objective a true *lebensraum*, the *limes* and boundaries of which march with and impinge upon mundane lands, but which had extending frontiers the other side of time. (*EA*, 259)

We recall that 'Lance-Corporal Aneirin Merddyn Lewis had somewhere in his Welsh depths a remembrance of the nature of man', and it should now be clear what this means. Man's 'native *Raum*', his 'double home-land', is the march land of matter of spirit, and time and eternity. This is the domain of 'Brut's Albion', of the Island kept within the Christian culture of the West by the Romano-Welsh and their descendants, a culture with a sacred history connecting it to the beginning of human life on earth. This is the realm of 'Arthur the Protector of the Land, the Leader, the Saviour, the Lord of Order carrying a raid into the place of Chaos', Arthur the sleeping Lord, for whom the Welsh hills are 'his couch / or is he the couchant hills?' (*SL*, 96). It was thus one of Jones's aims to subvert the narrow space of 'Engle-raum', closed to the older tradition of the Island, by restoring the deep things of 'Brut's Albion'. Cultural restoration, by things working up from under, is thus effected by analogy with the neurotic mind that is made whole by returning to its beginnings.

At this point in considering Jones's idea of 'the unity of this island', to which, he says, 'the Welsh, however separatist by historical, racial and geographical accidents, are devoted', we are faced, I think, by two alternative temptations. One is to take the part of the fact-man and dismiss it as fantasy. The other is to translate it into the terms of a specific political programme: the Welsh nationalism espoused by Saunders Lewis, that pleaded for 'the principle of unity and diversity', and fought for 'the civilisation of Wales'[8] and her place in Europe.

It will be evident from this paper which of the two temptations I lean towards. But I think it has to be refused. What we have to recognize is the kind of poet Jones was: that he expressed the tensions and conflicts of his time, dramatized the questions, but did not presume to provide answers. As he said of Southey's lines ''Tis some poor fellow's skull, said he', and 'But 'twas a famous victory' and Aneirin's 'His sword rang in mothers' heads': 'We share the conflicting and unresolved emotions . . . for the sixth century no less than the eighteenth shared our dilemma. And it is the business of a poet in the sixth, or eighteenth, or any century, to express the dilemma, not to comment upon it, or pretend to a solution' (*DG*, 130).

'It is the business of a poet . . . to express the dilemma'. It should be helpful, finally, to juxtapose this idea with another. Of his material Jones wrote: 'one is trying to make a shape out of the very things of which one is oneself made' (*A*, 10). In his case, the things included his father's *patria*. But his sense of 'belonging' to his 'father's people and their land' was inseparable from his dilemma as a religious artist in a secular epoch, and a Londoner who was attached to Wales. This is why I have to qualify what I said earlier in comparing his images of Welsh land and culture to J. R. Jones's idea of *cydymdreiddiad*. It is true that the latter was formulated in response to a situation of crisis, with the erosion of the culture of Welsh-speaking Wales in the twentieth century, but it was born of the experience of living in Wales. Jones's ideas, on the other hand, are better understood in the context of a statement made in his essay 'Wales and Visual Form', written in 1944: 'We all are as uprooted as the nation of the Jews and that is why we weep when we remember Sion – the old local Sions with their variants of the form-creating human cultures. We are all of the diaspora now' (*DG*, 88). It is to this very uprootedness that we owe Jones's sense of the matter of Wales. He described the art of James Joyce as 'showing an essential Celticity'.

Joyce's art was

> forged in exile by a man of our placeless cosmopolis, yet an art wholly
> determined by place, a place, an exact site, an art which, for its *materia
> poetica*, employs stuff from all the strata and the flux, from before and
> before again, to weave a word-web, a sound-web, round the 'Town of the
> Ford of Hurdles' as Dublin was called by the Goidels. (*DG*, 58)

It may be that Jones exaggerated our placelessness; but it was what he
came to feel. And we owe to it, paradoxically, as he says of Joyce, some
of the richest invocations of place in his work – the London of the Lady
of the Pool, for example, and the prayer of a Celt to the Tutelar of the
Place – a prayer which he will not permit us to think of 'as a pleading
for anything on my part':[9]

> In the bland megalopolitan light
>> where no shadow is by day or by night
> be our shadow.
> Remember the mound-kin, the kith of the *tarren* gone from this moun-
> tain because of the exorbitance of the Ram ... remember them in the
> rectangular tenements, in the houses of the engines that fabricate the
> ingenuities of the Ram ... Mother of Flowers save them then where no
> flower blows.
>
> . . .
>
> In all times of *Gleichschaltung*, in the days of the central economies,
> set up the hedges of illusion round some remnant of us, twine the
> wattles of mist, white-web a Gwydion-hedge
>> like fog on the *bryniau*
>> against the commissioners
> and assessors bearing the writs of the Ram to square the world-floor
> and number the tribes and write down the secret things and take away
> the diversities by which we are ...
>
> . . .
>
> Sweet Mair devise a mazy-guard
> in and out and round about
> double-dance defences
> countermure and echelon meanders round
> the holy mound ... (*SL*, 63–4)

We may be forbidden by the author to think of this as *his* pleading, as
his prayer for Wales, for example. It is, however, a Welsh landscape
around which he weaves 'a word-web, a sound-web', a landscape of

memory and magic, a homeland 'where matter marches with spirit', and the tutelary figure is 'Sweet Mair'.

The life of the work of a great writer reveals different things to different readers at the same time, and other things again to readers at other times, depending upon their sensibilities and the questions they ask of it. I am fully aware that this paper is a partial account of one important aspect of Jones, and by no means says all there is to say about his concern with the matter of Wales. With this in mind, I would like to end by making two general points.

The first concerns patriotism. *In Parenthesis* and *The Anathemata* were both responses to critical periods in modern British history, to war, and the rise of a utilitarian civilization inimical to the survival of local cultures. Neither is chauvinistic, but both express their author's love of the things of the Island of Britain. The overall effect of this emphasis is to put England in its place, in several senses. *The Anathemata* relates the making of the British people to the making of the land itself. It celebrates

> The adaptations, the fusions
> the transmogrifications
>   but always
> the inward continuities
>   of the site
>   of place. (90)

It shows the English as one element of a diverse culture with roots in an ancient unity, a unity that state policy since the Tudors, indeed since the death of Llywelyn in 1282, has been to suppress. One may quarrel with Jones's ideas about history; it is the expression of a profoundly humane love of country which, in the context of narrow English sympathies, makes his poetry liberating.

Some may feel that Jones, in his historical preoccupations, largely ignores the world since the Reformation, thus invalidating claims that his major writings include history, and can therefore be described, in Ezra Pound's terms, as epics. In fact, however, he does not ignore the modern world. On the contrary, he writes with an acute sense of its dilemmas. One of his main concerns is empire – the British Empire, which he treats through the analogy of the Roman Empire, and the conflict within the imperial and post-imperial period between the civilization that imposes a uniform world-plan and the life and values of small cultures and nations. He does not resolve the conflict; he writes as a man who knows it in his own mind and body. That is one reason why he speaks to us, because the conflict is, in different situations, central to the modern experience. We may feel – I do feel – an uneasiness about his thinking in terms of race, especially in view of its potential exclusiveness in a Britain that can no longer be said to be composed by the elements of '*gens, Volk, cenedl*' (*A*, 241). To dwell on this tendency in his work, however, let alone to associate it with the murderous consequences of a preoccupation with blood and soil, is to be dead to its generous and humane spirit, indeed its universal inclusiveness. In Britain, and in many other parts of the world, individuals and peoples know life in the present as a state of tension and conflict between attachment to an original 'home' and the coercive or attractive powers that create disruption, movement, change. In his ambivalent attachments as a Welshman and a Londoner, as well as in other respects, Jones lived the history of his time. In his writing and art he addressed a crisis which, manifested in the local and particular, has profound implications for human identity and the survival of the creative principle.

Notes

[1] See for example Saunders Lewis's 'An Introduction to David Jones's Dream of Private Clitus', in Aneirin Talfan Davies, *David Jones: Letters to a Friend* (Swansea: Christopher Davies, 1980).

[2] 'A Note of Introduction', in *In Parenthesis* (London: Faber, paperback edition, 1963), p. vii.

[3] Davies, *David Jones: Letters*, pp.115–16.

[4] See for example his comments on Artio, 'the female bear-deity of pre-history', in 'The Myth of Arthur', in *Epoch and Artist*, pp.232–3.

[5] See *Epoch and Artist*, p.243.

[6] *The Itinerary Through Wales and the Description of Wales* (London: J. M. Dent, Everyman's Library, 1908), p.205.

[7] Ned Thomas discusses the idea of *cydymdreiddiad* in *Derek Walcott: Poet of the Islands* (Cardiff: Welsh Arts Council, 1980), p.15.

[8] The quotations from Saunders Lewis are taken from Dafydd Glyn Jones's essay on Lewis's politics, in Alun R. Jones and Gwyn Thomas (eds.), *Presenting Saunders Lewis* (Cardiff: University of Wales Press, 1973), p.29.

[9] Davies, *David Jones: Letters*, p.37.

The Scapebeast

WILLIAM BLISSETT

'Scapebeast': the word was coined by David Jones on the model of 'scapegoat'. We shall be considering pictorial and literary representations of animals that bear a burden of meaning and impose a duty of interpretation, but before doing so it will be salutary to recall Jones's drawing of a goat in which there is nothing ethically problematical, nothing demonic, no imputed guilt. It must stand for a rich and various gallery of such animals, such goats, beginning with one of the treasures of the British Museum, a figure of a goat, made of shell, lapis lazuli and gold, from Ur of the Chaldees, about 2500 BC: it is standing boldly, nibbling a tree. To these might be added a Peruvian alpaca in Inca silver, a frisky Capricorn from a fourteenth-century Bohemian manuscript, and Picasso's *Girl with a Goat*, in the Barnes Collection. All these are works of art, set apart as 'anathemata', and all bear the artist's 'sign-manual', whether his name is known or not. I mention them thus prominently for their own beautiful sakes and as a needed reminder not to find the scapegoat in every representation of a goat. Of course, they are to be interpreted, accounted for, but there is nothing 'literary' about them, in any of the senses applicable to David Jones and to Holman Hunt before him and Robert Rauschenberg after, in their varied treatments of the scapebeast.

There is always a buzz of confusion around any living symbol. Most of us would recognize and use the word 'scapegoat' not in a closely defined neutral sense but in a vague but highly charged, highly political, sacred and profane sense – seriously, to apply to victims of persecution; less seriously, to apply to embarrassed public figures or losers of crucial games. We do this usually without recalling the original scapegoat of Leviticus, chapter 16.

On the Great Day of Atonement, Yom Kippur, Aaron the High Priest, having offered sacrifice for himself and his house, receives two goats from the assembled people:

7 And he shall take the two goats, and present them before the LORD at the door of the tabernacle of the congregation.

8 And Aaron shall cast lots upon the two goats; one lot for the LORD, and the other lot for the scapegoat.

9 And Aaron shall bring the goat upon which the LORD'S lot fell, and offer him for a sin offering.

10 But the goat, on which the lot fell to be the scapegoat, shall be presented alive before the LORD, to make an atonement with him, and to let him go for a scapegoat into the wilderness.

Then, after prescribing the rite of sacrifice at the altar of the first goat (strictly, the victim), the passage continues:

21 And Aaron shall lay both his hands upon the head of the live goat, and confess over him all the iniquities of the children of Israel, and all their transgressions in all their sins, putting them on the head of the goat: and shall send him away by the hand of a fit man into the wilderness.

22 And this goat shall bear upon him all their iniquities unto a land not inhabited: and he shall let the goat go in the wilderness.

The name and nature of the scapegoat derive from this passage, and serious discourse should not permit radical departure from the meaning of the rite it prescribes.

A number of observations may be drawn from this text, fleshed out somewhat by adding to the bare bones of the rite some time-honoured exegetical commentary.[1]

It will be observed that time and place are defined and localized. The expulsion of the scapegoat takes place at a yearly rite of great solemnity, and at no other time, from the Temple itself, in the presence of the High Priest and the assembled people. Two and only two goats are selected; since one is to be offered up, both must be young, unblemished, acceptable as a sacrifice, and since one is to be ejected, both must be rejectable. These roles are assigned by lot, that is by the will of God, not by the merit of contest or by the popularity of acclamation. Though kosher, neither goat provides a feast. The sacrificed goat is a sin offering and therefore is entirely consumed by fire. As a priestly people, Israel, to offer such sacrifice must separate itself from sin; the scapegoat, now blemished by imputation, is the sin from which the people separate themselves, and hence, far from being a feast, it is an image of dearth and want and is ejected to die in that role. He has the sins of the people laid on his head and is marked by a scarlet cloth on his horns: he may be mocked, cursed, buffeted, but the mistreatment should be token, for the shedding of blood in the city would be polluting, and he must live to carry his load out of the city. He is conveyed by a guard to prevent his return: pushing him over a cliff to certain death belongs to the end of the tradition when meaning is blurred and practical concerns crowd in. Left to perish, he is subsumed to the howling wilderness.[2]

To repeat with emphasis a point now regularly lost sight of: the scapegoat is in no sense a sacrificial victim. The marks of an acceptable or auspicious sacrifice, we recall from classical as well as biblical records, are that the animal, healthy and sound, should be well treated and garlanded, going to the place of immolation without a struggle, as if willingly. It is particularly auspicious if it can be persuaded to nod its head. It is victimized, certainly, but not persecuted. The scapegoat in contrast is not oblated or immolated but ejected: as it were, excreted from the body politic, he passes to the dunghill of undoing. That is why he should not bleed and must not die until he reaches the point of no return. A further observation is that, after reading the *Scapegoat* volume of Sir James Frazer's *Golden Bough* (as David Jones did early in life),[3] with its circumstantial accounts of myriads of heathenish rites and customs, many of them cruel, disgusting and irrational, one returns to the original Judaic ritual to find it in a class by itself for clarity and control. The context is penitential, not orgiastic; the sacrificial victim and the scapegoat, distinct as they are, relate closely by being opposites, the one offered up, the other cast out, the offering being central to the rite, the ejection peripheral. One is made much of, the other is made

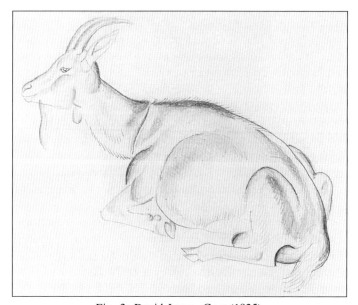

Fig. 2: David Jones, *Goat* (1925)

nothing of; one belongs on the right hand, in the Temple, the other on the left, in the wilderness. The imputation of sin and the expulsion of the goat are deliberate, rational, limited, virtual. If far removed from heathendom, how much farther from what we loosely call 'scapegoating' – the witch-hunts, lynchings and pogroms, malicious and sporadic, that accurately symptomize the maladies of societies, especially Christian societies. Being a book of rituals, Leviticus tells you only what you must do, not what you must think or how you must feel. One might say 'poor beast' or one might say 'good riddance', but the intention of the rite is that one should see in the animal only the sins of the people (including one's own), confessed, repented, abandoned. It is a day to afflict oneself, or the whole point of the rite is lost in the scuffle.[4]

I have quoted the Authorized Version, which follows the Latin Vulgate, which in turn follows the Septuagint, the Greek scriptures of Judaism. The Revised Standard Version and most other modern translations follow the original Hebrew and leave the word we are used to as 'scapegoat' untranslated as the proper name Azazel. 'Scapegoat'[5] seems to have been a word invented by William Tyndale in 1530 to translate the Vulgate *caper emissarius*, goat to be sent out (French, *bouc émissaire*). The Hebrew contrasts the goat sacrificed to the Lord as a sin offering, with the goat ejected as a sin bearer, sent to Azazel, who seems to have been, even among evil spirits, a shadowy figure, haunting and personifying the empty and arid waste land, the outer darkness. There is not the least suggestion of two parallel sacrifices, for one of them would be idolatrous, and the God of Israel is a jealous God. A sacrifice is an oblation, something offered up, a vessel of honour, of imputed innocence, an image of value, of the worshipper's best self. A scapegoat is ejected, a vessel of dishonour, of imputed guilt, an image of no value, of a person's worst self. Sending the goat to Azazel is keeping Azazel at a distance: nobody himself, nothingness, *le néant, das Nichts*, he is allowed to feed on the negativities of sin.

The animal to which sin is imputed is a goat, not a bull or a lamb or a dove (to mention other creatures acceptable as sacrifices). The fact that the goat is kosher is no guarantee of its moral character. The kid in fact and fable is lively and frolicsome, more boisterous than the lamb but hardly less innocent. The adult animal has a pungent personality, a loud stink. The he-goat may not be any more highly sexed than the stud horse, the bull, the ram, but he reeks of sex, and his face has a lustful leer. The jealous Othello exclaims 'Goats and monkeys!' Moreover, the goat is omnivorous with a vengeance: feeding on roots and bark and cropping close, he is hard on the environment, a desert-maker. 'The goat coughs at night in the field overhead; / Rocks, moss, stonecrop, iron, merds.'[6] The Greek for goat, *tragos*, has the Indo-European root TR in it, associated with destructive gnawing – as in at*t*rition, *t*ribulation, *t*ermite. (By the way, we get *tragedy* from 'goatsong', because the goat as an enemy of the vine was sacred-accursed to Dionysus.) The goat, then, in look and behaviour, is a good figure of reprobation – not particularly fierce or dangerous, but stubborn, mean, destructive, cussed. The New Testament image of the sheep and the goats derives from the practical necessity of keeping the two herds separate, but anyone who didn't know could easily guess which belongs on the right hand and which on the left. The least domesticated of domestic animals, the goat belongs at the margin of the wilderness; the sheep only strays there. Goats are not stabled but may be penned. I have not found goats among the harmless beasts in scenes of the Nativity.

II

The goat-footed satyrs of antiquity frolicked with nymphs and fauns and danced the antic hay, but their great god Pan represented the All, and with it the terrifying Unbounded, the cause of panic. And so, when it came time to represent the Evil One in the Christian world, the image of the goatish daemonic figure lay handy. Suspected witches were to be examined for horns and cloven feet before expulsion from panic-stricken communities.[7]

One would think that there would be a rich and varied literary and pictorial record of the scapegoat theme, connecting it with the goat-devil and the goat-witch, but one would be wrong. Two Romantic poets may be seen as inaugurating the loose modern sense of the scapegoat 'victim' or 'sacrifice', individual or collective. Lord Byron, who had a deformed foot and enjoyed being thought wicked, made a sort of trade mark of his cloven hoof and paraded his expulsion from society. He as much as says 'Call me Cain' as, a generation later the narrator of *Moby Dick* comes out and says 'Call me Ishmael'. Alfred de Vigny in 1835, pondering on the great armies maintained after the Napoleonic Wars, observed that

> the enlisted man, the soldier, is both pathetic and heroic, both executioner and victim, a scapegoat [*bouc émissaire*] fooled by the public to whom and in whose stead he is daily sacrificed; he is a martyr at once fierce and mild, torn between the discordant interests of the nation and the sovereign power.

Note that the yearly and special has become daily, quotidian. This is perhaps the earliest, certainly the first memorable use of *scapegoat* to apply to a wide category of disadvantaged persons.[8]

But it was William Holman Hunt (1827–1910), an original member with Dante Gabriel Rossetti and John Everett Millais of the Pre-Raphaelite Brotherhood, who with earnest Victorian dedication went to the Holy Land and there painted the literal scapegoat for the first time in the history of art.

The larger of its two versions, in the Lady Lever Gallery, Port Sunlight, is the more famous and will concern us. Dated OOSDOOM DEAD SEA 1854 (note the overtones of 'doom' and 'Sodom'), its very frame is a sermon, having, above, seven stars and the words from Isaiah (applying to the Suffering Servant recognized by Christians as a type of Christ), 'Surely he hath borne our Griefs, and carried away our Sorrows: / yet we did esteem him stricken, smitten of God, and afflicted.' Below, a seven-branched candlestick and the title THE SCAPE-GOAT, with the text, 'And the goat shall bear upon him all their Iniquities unto a Land not inhabited.'

The painting itself (Fig. 3) is luminous, even hectic, in colour. The band above the horns, stretching to the reflected moon on the salt surface to the left, is opalescent, as is the sky above the mountains. Contrast the dull salt ground under the goat's feet, the base of the mountains, and the slate-green strip of the sea. The rib-cage of an animal, right centre, picks up the lines of the goat's form; the bifurcated branch, left centre, is horn-like. A skull, bottom left, stares blindly at the goat's head. The twigs and debris, bottom right, might be droppings of an animal. The goat is the only living thing in

Fig. 3: William Holman Hunt, *The Scapegoat* (1854)
(Merseyside County Art Galleries)

an environment fiercely hostile to life; relics of previous life are scattered about. The only man-made thing is the red garland on the goat's horns, emblematic of the scarlet sins to be bleached white as wool, and that is the only colour that is not mineral and poisonous.

On his return from the Holy Land, Hunt encountered widespread incomprehension, first from his dealer, who had never heard of scape-goats.[9] The painting was exhibited, and received a good deal of attention. The clergy, including some bishops, liked it, so that the artist 'wished that their stipends had been large enough to enable them to become patrons'. Oddly, the question one would think bound to arise for the earnest Victorians seems not to have occurred to them. What is the ethical status of the painter and the viewer in relation to the suffering and abandoned animal? Is it good for us to be here as onlookers, appre-ciating the brushwork and the scriptural typology, while the creature perishes, without even bearing the High Priest's imputation of our sins? It is comforting to know that Holman Hunt as a matter of fact took good care of his goats (the first one died), but the question comes back to haunt us.

The picture continues to be problematical. Simply as a happening it is astounding: it stops the casual gallery-goer dead in his tracks. Sir John Rothenstein in his history of British art regarded it as a landmark in its time; Graham Reynolds in *Victorian Painting* called it 'one of the most conspicuous eyesores in nineteenth-century art' – which should give it some status in the late twentieth century, the heyday of the eyesore. Recently Robert Harbison had this to say of it: Hunt

> proposes that medieval arbitrariness of symbolic equivalence should go together with modern arbitrariness of mechanical reproduction . . . Thus one is left with a world which falls apart into appearance and meaning, where one cannot turn, as medieval artists could, to an image which means better for not looking like what one sees.[10]

If the biblical scapegoat enters English art in the pictures of Holman Hunt, he enters English literature in a poem by Robert Graves, 'In the Wilderness', published in his first collection, *Over the Brazier* (1916), and his second, *Fairies and Fusiliers* (1917), and subsequently as the opening poem in retrospective collections throughout his long life. Graves and Jones were both born in 1895 and both served in the Royal Welch Fusiliers, Graves as an officer, Jones as a private. They never met, but their careers afford many pertinent parallels and contrasts, as I am attempting to show in another study. Like Jones, Graves was an early reader of Frazer and might have known that the *Scapegoat* volume of *The Golden Bough* was originally announced as 'The Man of Sorrows'. The poet who is later to write *King Jesus* and *The Nazarene Gospel Restored* begins his poem:

> He, of his gentleness,
> Thirsting and hungering
> Walked in the wilderness ...

and continues:

> Then ever with him went,
> Of all his wanderings
> Comrade, with ragged coat.
> Gaunt ribs – poor innocent –
> Bleeding foot, burning throat,
> The guileless young scapegoat ...[11]

III

David Jones, unlike Holman Hunt, made the transition to the modern – that 'image which means better for not looking like what one sees'. He grew up on the Pre-Raphaelites, whose influence and 'look' must have been pervasive in his youth. A small matter: he kept their slang, referring to beautiful women as 'stunners' and to ready cash as 'tin'; a great matter: he shared (though very differently understood) their deepest convictions about the religious basis of art.

Like Hunt, Jones journeyed to the Holy Land, in 1934, and this experience influenced all his subsequent writing, though not his painting. The howling wilderness he knew directly was not on the shores of the Dead Sea but in the trenches and no-man's-land of the Western Front. In the Preface to *In Parenthesis* he writes:

> I think the day by day in the Waste Land, the sudden violences and the long stillnesses, the sharp contours and unformed voids of that mysterious existence, profoundly affected the imaginations of those who suffered it. It was a place of enchantment. It is perhaps best described in Malory, book iv, chapter 15 – that landscape spoke 'with a grimly voice ...'(*IP*, x–xi)

He goes on to say, 'I had intended to engrave some illustrations, but have been prevented' (xiii). We do have two in the book, a frontispiece (fig. 4) and a tail-piece (fig. 5). The frontispiece shows a young soldier in a ravaged landscape, shattered trees and details of men in the background,

Fig. 4: David Jones, Frontispiece to *In Parenthesis* (1937)

the ever-present rat in the foreground. The soldier, except for the remnants of uniform and impedimenta on his right shoulder, is stripped naked, bruised and lacerated, vulnerable from all sides, his arms suggesting the crucifixion they awkwardly attempt to ward off. The impossibility of his either remaining in that position or changing it makes our bones ache. For all its realistic detail of spade, barbed wire and trench, this is a thoroughly modern picture, with its multiple perspective, its deliberate selection and distortion.

We are likely to say, too easily, 'a Christ figure', and to recall the often-quoted passage from a letter of Wilfred Owen, July 1918:

> For fourteen hours yesterday I was at work – teaching Christ to lift his cross by numbers, and how to adjust his crown; and not to imagine he thirst until after the last halt; I attended his Supper to see that there were no complaints; and inspected his feet to see that they should be worthy of the nails. I see to it that he is dumb and stands to attention before his accusers. With a piece of silver I buy him every day, and with maps I make him familiar with the topography of Golgotha.

Fig. 5: David Jones, *The Victim*, Tailpiece to
In Parenthesis (1937)

David Jones, who admired Owen and thought his poems, written at the Front, 'a unique and marvellous achievement' was troubled by this. He wrote, in a letter to René Hague, July 1973:

> ... I don't like his identification of the grimly circumstances and maims and 'dole and tray and tene' with the Passion of the Incarnate Logos – yes the bit you quote from the letter is an astonishing *tour de force* and, as you say, 'terrific'. But none the less, I don't like the analogy ...[12]

His misgivings are like those that some of us feel with the arguments of René Girard in *Violence and the Sacred* and *The Scapegoat*, the latter book, despite its title, making no distinction between sacrificial victim and scapegoat.[13]

The tailpiece stands at the close of the book, facing a page of scriptural texts in Roman capitals. One recalls the presence of texts on the frame of Holman Hunt's *Scapegoat*. I will give them, in translation when necessary. They seem to apply as much to the frontispiece as to the tailpiece: it is of course intended that the reader of them will have seen both and read the book:

AND I SAW ... THE LAMB STANDING AS IT HAD BEEN SLAIN.

THE GOAT ON WHICH THE LOT FELL LET HIM GO FOR A SCAPE-GOAT INTO THE WILDERNESS

WHAT IS THY BELOVED MORE THAN ANOTHER BELOVED?

HE HATH NO FORM NOR COMELINESS: AND WHEN WE SHALL SEE HIM, THERE IS NO BEAUTY THAT WE SHOULD DESIRE HIM.

YOUR LAMB SHALL BE WITHOUT BLEMISH, A MALE OF THE FIRST YEAR.

THIS IS MY BELOVED AND THIS IS MY FRIEND.[14]

In the midst of the text, but reaching back and ahead to the two illustrations, is this crucial passage:

> But these [soldiers] sit in the wilderness, pent like lousy rodents all the day long, appointed scape-beasts come to the waste-lands, to grope, to stumble at the margin of familiar things – at the place of separation ...
>
> And with the night comes the dark meeting [in no-man's-land] of these by lot chosen – each the Azazel to each, other demon drawn to other. (*IP*, 70)

The key word, of course, is the one he coined – 'scape-beast'. He knows the difference between sheep and goats, and between the sacrificial victim and the scapegoat, the oblation and immolation of the one, the ejection under curse of the other. He knows the name and nature of Azazel. Cain and Abel he also understands when he writes of

> Each one bearing in his body the whole apprehension of that innocent, on the day he saw his brother's votive smoke diffuse and hang to soot the fields of holocaust; neither approved nor ratified nor made acceptable but lighted to everlasting partition. (*IP*, 162)

And again,

> ... it will be him and you in an open place, he will look into your face; fear will so condition you that you each will pale for the other, and in one another you will hate your own flesh. (*IP*, 121)

Jones himself is not confused, though the war itself is a tornado of confusion, with its hecatombs of victims, its deafening prate about sacrifice, its pharmaceutical promises of some final catharsis at the expulsion of the Hun, the militarist, of War itself. What he wants is fusion not confusion, to achieve in image and metaphor a unity unachievable in concept or argument. He will point to this operation later when he invents and exalts the 'Anathemata' – the word, the idea, the 'thing': whatever is set apart and signed. How far removed is this from the crudities of BLAST and BLESS, and how much wiser the quiet *fauve* of *In Parenthesis* than the noisy *fauve* of *Blasting and Bombardiering*.

In the tailpiece the primary reference is to the ram caught in the thicket that provided Abraham with a sacrificial victim to substitute for Isaac. The victim, in contrast to the soldier of the frontispiece, holds himself not dejectedly but with proud innocency, but he is a victim not in a sanctified place but in the scapegoat's world of dereliction, the 'loveless scene' (*IP*, 75). When a corporal comes to detail some men for a fatigue, one exclaims, 'Here comes bloody Anti-Christ with a packet for each us'n's', and another caps it with 'Sheep nor goats dont signify' (*IP*, 114). They certainly signify elsewhere in the text: we need only recall Lt Jenkins, so often compared to a shepherd tending his company, his 'armed bishopric', and how as his last command in battle he shouts out, 'and don't bunch on the left for Christ's sake' (*IP*, 160). A faint echo from early in the book may reach across to this place of dereliction – 'Left be buggered' (*IP*, 36).

David Jones took a keen interest in the history and traditions of the Royal Welch Fusiliers, but one ritual he never mentions in his writings.

The mascot of the regiment is a goat, which is brought into the officers' mess once a year, on St David's Day, suitably doused in eau-de-Cologne. In the context of the book it would have detracted from the pervasive image of the scapegoat and seemed forced, capricious. It was an officers' ritual and this is an enlisted man's book; and compared to the cosseted animal any enlisted man was despised and rejected.

His feeling for the fate of animals comes out in other ways. The horses: 'these dumb, who seem to sense how they perish with this flesh – their whinneying so pitiable' (*IP*, 111); the mules: 'and mules died: their tough clipt hides that have a homely texture flayed horribly to make you weep, sunk in their servility of chain and leather' (*IP*, 149). When he was writing *In Parenthesis* and beginning to think of 'The Book of Balaam's Ass', he used to go to the zoo and draw animals, and these (including the untroubled goat) are placid and self-contained. But as a child he had drawn a dancing bear, muzzled, chained, and thwarted of its nature, and as an old man confined to a single room he had on his wall a newspaper clipping of the Russian dog Laika that had been blasted to the wilderness of outer space.[15]

The complex theme we have been looking at persists in the work of David Jones, unobtrusively in the writing, strongly in the pictures. When in *The Anathemata* he gives examples of 'unshared backgrounds' that need annotation, one of the first four he cites is Azazel (*A*, 14). The doomed soldiers of Passchendaele are called 'shopkeepers in scapegoat hauberks' (*SL*, 99); and in 'The Agent', the Judas fragment in the posthumously edited *Roman Quarry*, one finds 'we need an *azazel*' (*RQ*, 149), 'a goat's a goat, the lot's on him' (*RQ*, 150), and (alluding to the Roman expulsion ritual) 'or do we chase the old Mars out' (*RQ*, 152).

One of his finest copper engravings shows the Ancient Mariner with the albatross hung from his neck; *In Parenthesis* was begun as the *Mariner* plates were being designed, and the book is full of Mariner echoes, and at the end the wounded John Ball feels his rifle 'to hang at your bowed neck like the Mariner's white oblation' (*IP*, 184). In the *Book of Jonah* the hard-pressed mariners cast lots to find the accursed one who brought the storm upon them. The lot falls on Jonah, and he is cast into the watery wilderness. The depiction of the cruciform ejection of the prophet stands as one of Jones's most powerful wood engravings.

One last quotation, emphatic in its brevity: writing to his friend Desmond Chute, a priest, who had years before taught him the basic art of wood engraving, David Jones says, 'as far as I can see, "man the artist" and "man the priest" become increasingly, in a sense, Ishmaels, or men of a kind of diaspora, within our technological set-up.'[16]

IV

In 1955 the American painter Robert Rauschenberg began a work that still stands at the centre of his fame (fig. 6). He acquired a 'horned, long-haired Angora goat' from a second-hand furniture store:

> its fleece was matted with decades of dust and its face bashed in on one side. He spent hours cleaning the fleece with dog shampoo, and he fixed up the face as best he could; the damage was still apparent, though, and for this reason he decided to cover it with paint. 'So many people ask me why I put that awful paint on his face,' he said once. 'It's what seems to bother them the most.' The real problem, though, was to make the animal look as though it belonged in a painting.

This problem he solved by placing the goat in the middle of a 'flat, horizontal platform, painted and collaged in his usual manner', so as to make 'an environment, a place for him to be, a pasture'.[17]

The construct is much written on, much talked of: like Holman Hunt's *Scapegoat* it arrests the gallery-goer. I have seen it twice in the Stockholm Museum of Modern Art, and found it challenging, moving, even haunting. Why so? The context of this question should be fully in place, and so the answer presents itself promptly and baldly: it is the

Fig. 6: Robert Rauschenberg, *Monogram* (1959)
(Statens Konstmuseer – The National Swedish Art Museums)

scapegoat for our time. The paint on the face is the garlanding of the horns made new, a marking with a sign-manual, a setting apart as anathemata. And the rubber tyre? Just as David Jones impaled his scapebeast on the barbed wire of the Western Front, so Rauschenberg impales and dishonours his animal with the junk of urban industrialism. And his 'pasture'? Dry as the Dead Sea, cluttered as no-man's-land, more meagre than either.

In conclusion, we may well recall, with only a minimum of comment, one other image, a very famous one, much copied by art students. A Roman copy of a Greek original at Pergamum, it serves as frontispiece and gives its name to the posthumous collection of Jones's essays, *The Dying Gaul*. 'I naturally liked him, for he epitomized for me so much of Celtdom, or what little I knew of it in 1909–10. At least I sensed a continuity of struggle and a continuity of loss' (*DG*, 26). Jones appropriated it for life. Years later, in the Roman fragments of *The Sleeping Lord*, he returns to the figure again and again. In 'The Wall', gladiatorial shows are evoked:

> All should turn out to see how those appointed to die take the Roman medicine. They crane their civvy necks half out their civvy suits to bait the maimed king in his tinctured vesture, the dying *tegernos* of the wasted *landa* well webbed in our marbled parlour, bitched and bewildered and far from his dappled patria far side the misted Fretum . . . (*SL*, 11)

and, before the end of the fragment (with sharp irony),

> now all can face the dying god
> the dying Gaul
> without regret (*SL*, 14)

The 'scapebeast' returns in 'The Fatigue' (*SL*, 34), and the sardonic, despairing Tribune can recall 'the April mocked man' and the 'dying Gaul' (*SL*, 46, 53). There is a final, daring, Joycean play in the title poem, a last jab at the Ram and and Zone and the technological society:

> Or, is the dying gull
>   on her sea-hearse
> that drifts the oily bourne
>   to tomb at turn of tide
> her own stricken cantor? (*SL*, 93)

Notes

[1] I have consulted a number of commentaries on the passage: Bernard J. Bamberger, *The Torah* (New York: Union of Hebrew Congregations, 1970), III, pp.160–1; R. J. Faley, 'Scapegoat', in *New Catholic Encyclopedia* (New York: McGraw-Hill, 1967); R. K. Harrison, *Leviticus: An Introduction* (Leicester: Inter-Varsity Press, 1986), pp.170–3; *Interpreter's Bible* (New York: Abingdon, 1953), II, pp.77–85; *New Interpreter's Bible* (1994), I, pp.1111–12; J. A. Noordtij, *Leviticus* (Grand Rapids: Zondervan, 1982), pp.160–3; Martin Noth, *Leviticus* (Philadelphia: Westminster, 1965), pp.124–5; Ramban [Nachmanides], ed. and tr. Charles B. Chavel, *Commentary on the Torah* (New York: Shilo, 1974), pp.217–25.

[2] The 'howling wilderness' (Deut. 32:10), a great phrase on which there is little commentary. It enters Christian worship in the majestic hymn, 'The God of Abraham praise', which originated in the synagogue.

[3] David Jones said that 'the full, not the abridged Frazer is the thing to read: most of the good of it is in the notes and documentation.' See William Blissett, *The Long Conversation* (London: Oxford University Press, 1981), p.96. He possessed two copies of the abridgement, but also *Adonis* (1932), *Adonis, Attis, Osiris* (1906, acquired 1951), *The Dying God* (1912), *Psyche's Task* (1920, acquired 1951), and *The Scapegoat* (1914). See Huw Ceiriog Jones (ed.), *The Library of David Jones . . . A Catalogue* (Aberystwyth: National Library of Wales, 1995).

[4] The question of the Hellenic analogue to the Hebraic scapegoat – the 'pharmakos' – is too complex to be entered into here. An animal or (most usually) man is fêted and then driven out with abuse, thus purging the community. This often had an element of game and seldom resulted in death. See Walter Burkert, *Homo Necans*, tr. Peter Bing (Berkeley and Los Angeles: University of California Press, 1983) and *Structure and History in Greek Mythology and Ritual* (Berkeley and Los Angeles: University of California Press, 1979), pp.61–7; Jacques Derrida, 'Plato's Pharmacy', in *Disseminations*, tr. Barbara Johnson (Chicago: University of Chicago Press, 1981), pp.65–171; Dennis D. Hughes, *Human Sacrifice in Ancient Greece* (London: Routledge, 1991), pp.139–41, 164–5, 185–93; Robert Parker, *Miasma: Pollution and Purification in Early Greek Religion* (Oxford: Clarendon Press, 1983), pp.258–70, 322–7.

[5] The *OED*, which gives the Tyndale reference, also cites an astonishing sentence in Hobbes's *Leviathan* (xli): 'Christ is both the sacrificed goat and the Scape-goat.' The broader sense of 'one blamed or punished for the sins of others' dates only from Miss Mitford (1824) and Tennyson (1877), and the verb 'to scapegoat' is first found in the *Journal of Abnormal Psychology* in 1943.

[6] T. S. Eliot, 'Gerontion', *Collected Poems 1909–1962* (London: Faber, 1963), p.39.

[7] See Reinhard Herbig, *Pan der griechische Bocksgott* (Frankfurt: Klostermann, 1949); Patricia Merivale, *Pan the Goat-God* (Cambridge, Mass.: Harvard University Press, 1969); Elliott Rose, *A Razor for a Goat* (Toronto: University of Toronto Press, 1962); Beryl Rowland, *Animals with Human Faces* (Knoxville: University of Tennessee Press, 1973).

[8] Alfred de Vigny, *The Military Necessity*, tr. Humphrey House (London: Cresset Press, 1953), p.16.

[9] W. Holman Hunt, *Pre-Raphaelitism and the Pre-Raphaelite Brotherhood*

(London: Macmillan, 1905), II, pp.106–8. See also his 'Painting "The Scapegoat"', *Contemporary Review*, 52 (1887) 21–38, 206–20.

[10] Robert Harbison, *Deliberate Regression* (New York: Knopf, 1980), pp.157–60. For other discussions of Hunt's *Scapegoat*, see Archdeacon Farrar and Mrs Meynell, *William Holman Hunt: His Life and Work, The Art Annual* (1893), 12–16, with a photograph of Hunt while painting the picture; G. H. Fleming, *That Ne'er Shall Meet Again* (London: Michael Joseph, 1971), pp.17–19; Ford Madox Hueffer (later Ford), *Memories and Impressions* (New York: Harper, 1911), p.243: 'This is a terrifying and suggestive picture'; George P. Landow, *William Holman Hunt and Typological Symbolism* (New Haven: Yale University Press, 1979), pp.103–13; Martin Meisel, 'Seeing it Feelingly: Victorian Symbolism and Narrative Art', *Huntington Library Quarterly*, 49 (1986), 67–92, especially the connection with Rauschenberg, 88–9; Leslie Parris (ed.), *Pre-Raphaelite Papers* (London: Tate Gallery, 1984), for Judith Brockhurst, 'An Interesting Series of Adventures to Look Back Upon', pp.111–25; Graham Reynolds, *Victorian Painting* (London: Studio Vista, 1966), p.62; Allen Staley, *The Pre-Raphaelite Landscape* (Oxford: Clarendon Press, 1973), pp.66–9; Herbert Sussman, 'Hunt, Ruskin, and "The Scapegoat"', *Victorian Studies*, 12 (1968) 83–90.

[11] Robert Graves, 'In the Wilderness', in *Collected Poems* (London: Cassell, 1948), p.3. The 'old' scapegoat of the wartime printings is changed to 'young', at the dictate of truth; the poem is otherwise unchanged in the final collection of 1975, though Graves was aware of the practice of pushing the scapegoat over a cliff.

[12] Wilfred Owen, *Collected Letters*, ed. Harold Owen and John Bell (London: Oxford University Press, 1967), p.562, also pp.458–61; René Hague (ed.), *Dai Great-Coat* (London: Faber, 1980), p.245; see also Blissett, *Long Conversation*, p.58.

[13] René Girard, *Violence and the Sacred*, tr. Patrick Gregory (Baltimore: Johns Hopkins University Press, 1977), and *The Scapegoat*, tr. Yvonne Freccero (Baltimore: Johns Hopkins University Press, 1986). There are several wide-ranging collections of essays on the implications of Girard's thought, but see B. H. McLean, *The Cursed Christ: Mediterranean Expulsion Rituals and Pauline Soteriology* (Sheffield: Academic Press, 1996), a learned and cogent study.

[14] The passages are taken, in order, from Rev. 5:6; Lev. 16:10; S. of S. 5:9; Exod. 12:5; S. of S. 5:16. Jones did not continue the Exodus verse, which goes on: 'You shall take it [the paschal victim] out from the sheep or from the goats.'

[15] *The Fate of Animals* is the title of a (pre-war) painting by Franz Marc, a German painter killed on the Western Front. For Laika, my memory is confirmed by Kathleen Raine, *David Jones and the Actually Loved and Known* (Ipswich: Golgonooza Press, 1978), p.24.

[16] Thomas Dilworth (ed.), *Inner Necessities: The Letters of David Jones to Desmond Chute* (Toronto: Anson-Cartwright Editions, 1984), pp.25–6.

[17] Calvin Tomkins, *Off the Wall: Robert Rauschenberg and the Art World of our Time* (New York: Doubleday, 1980), pp.135–6.

David Jones and the
Maritain Conversation

THOMAS DILWORTH

In the preface to *The Anathemata*, Jones lists writers to whom he is
indebted. Topping the list are the French Jesuit theologian Maurice de
la Taille, the German culture-morphologist Oswald Spengler and the
French neo-Thomist philosopher Jacques Maritain. These three he
encountered in what were intellectually his most formative years, those
immediately following the Great War. As an influence, the greatest of
these is Maritain. Initially Maritain was so important to him because,
from early in 1919, Jones was suffering from post-war ennui involving a
crisis of vocation. All he had ever wanted to do was draw and paint, but
he could now see no significant relationship between art and the rest of
life. Art seemed meaningless. Maritain put an end to this crisis by defin-
ing for him the values of art and the relationship of art to its subject, to
the artist, to the 'consumer' of art, and to God. The influence of
Maritain was profound and enduring, because he defined for Jones what
art is, at its best, and described the life of the artist. There was nothing
prescriptive about this for Jones, who knew more about art than
Maritain, but Maritain provided for him a clear recognition of the truth
about art and about himself as an artist.

In August 1921, Jones met Eric Gill and Hilary Pepler, who were then
talking about the recently published *Art et Scholastique*, in which
Maritain elaborates on the aesthetic implications of medieval scholastic
thought, especially that of Aquinas. Excited by the affinities of
Maritain's book with the writings of Roger Fry, Gill and Pepler had
asked Father John O'Connor to translate it for publication by St
Dominic's Press. Gill was helping with the translation although he knew
very little French. (When Gill met Maritain on 10 September 1922, they
were unable to converse except through Gill's daughter Betty acting as
interpreter.) In January 1922, after being received into the Catholic
Church by O'Connor, Jones went to live with the tiny community of
workmen led by Gill and Pepler. Maritain's ideas were then their chief
intellectual preoccupation. Jones often spent much of the day and

evening discussing Maritain. O'Connor's translation was published under the title *The Philosophy of Art* in 1923, but by then its ideas had already informed a living stream of conversation for over a year. Eric Gill had directed and dominated the conversation. Jones would later acknowledge the 'very great value' for him of Gill's 'clarifying ideas', but many of those ideas were those of Maritain.[1] For Jones the source was unimportant: these ideas were not book-learned (he could not read French) but part of the fabric of his daily life. He did, of course, read O'Connor's translation, and he read it repeatedly. On 23 October 1923, he wrote to Gill from London, 'I have just finished re-reading the "Phl of Art" – it gets better each time I think.' He persuaded a former teacher to acquire it for the library of the Central School of Art and advised his friends to buy it, including one who said that it was, at that time, Jones's 'bible'.[2] Decades later Jones referred to it as 'greatly illuminating' and, according to his close friend Harman Grisewood, continued to 'venerate' it. He looked at the improved translation of the expanded version of 1930 but put it down, saying, 'I prefer O'Connor.'[3] In later years he referred more to works by other writers, but no other book meant as much to him. By the mid-1920s, its relationship to his mind resembled that of a map to a place.

His appreciation for the scope and penetration of Maritain's thought testifies to Jones's critical acuity, which owes a good deal to teaching by A. S. Hartrick and Walter Sickert. He was, however, fortunate to have encountered Maritain and to have been with others who realized Maritain's importance. This book was a seminal work of aesthetic theory. It would join the writing of Fry and Bell and the Russian and Czech formalists in generating a broad-based international formalist aesthetic that would inform mid-twentieth-century art theory and literary theory. This aesthetic would be an important contribution to western thought.

Maritain begins with the Aristotelian distinction between doing and making. For Jones, this distinction illuminated what he considered to be Gill's 'main contention': that modern scientific civilization was concerned only with doing, which Aristotle calls *praxis*, whereas man's special and proper activity is making, which Aristotle calls *poiesis*. Gill stressed this activity as distinctively human by repeatedly quoting the Thomistic definition of man as *homo faber*. About the basic distinction between kinds of activity, Jones would continue to think that Gill had 'fundamentally . . . got hold of a great truth'.[4] It was Maritain who had originally found this 'truth' in Aristotle, but Jones had first encountered it in conversation with Gill.

Maritain writes that doing is governed by the virtue of prudence and can be moral or immoral. In contrast, making is governed by Ars and is always amoral. The distinction effectively refuted for Jones the moralist objections to 'art for art's sake'. 'The artist, *qua* artist,' Jones later insisted, 'must know no conscience except with regard to the formal perfection of the work on hand – & there his conscience must be of the most scrupulous order.'[5]

In this context, amorality is an aspect of objectivity. The rules and values of art 'are not those of man', writes Maritain, 'but those of the work to be produced'.[6] However compelling the subjective feelings of the artist, he must detach himself from them during creation. Detachment is not denial: Jones asserted that strong feelings motivate the artist, but, he also wrote, 'the workman must be dead to himself while engaged upon the work, otherwise we have that sort of "self-expression" which is as undesirable in the painter or the writer as in the carpenter, the cantor, the half-back, or the cook' (*A*, 12). Maritain writes that the artist must also disregard 'the onlooker except to give him beauty', which means that the artist must not try to produce emotion, even delight. He must focus only on the thing he is making. This is the essence of artistic integrity, for which other artists and poets would admire Jones. As Gill put it, 'You must ask yourself, "Am I doing this because it is right, good and beautiful in itself, or because thus it pleases me or my customers that I should do it?"'[7] Ironically, Jones had serious reservations about Gill's erotic drawings and engravings precisely because they were evidently done to 'please' the artist and to arouse the 'customer'. Pornography, like political propaganda or commercialism (in which the primary purpose is profit), distorts art by diminishing aesthetic objectivity.

For its maker, art requires a pervasive mental disposition that intensifies perception and awareness, allowing an artist to *be* 'in some way' his work 'before it is done' (14). In other words – and A. S. Hartrick had impressed this upon Jones before the war – an artist must embody creative sensitivity, what Hartrick had called 'taste'. An artist has to be an unusual kind of person who, Maritain claims, 'sees deeper than others and . . . discovers in the concrete spiritual radiances, which others are unable to discern' (90). Jones was utterly convinced of all this in relation to himself. In 1962 he remarked about critical response to his paintings:

Chaps refer to the 'mystery' or 'subtlety' or 'illusiveness' or 'fragility' or 'waywardness' or 'complexity' or 'fancyfulness' etc., etc. – well, Christ almighty! what else is there in a bunch of flowers or a tree or a landscape or a girl or a sky but these qualities? By the severest logic one must somehow, if possible, capture something of these qualities if the thing is going to be any damn good. It isn't the artist's 'fancy' or 'imagination' that imposes these qualities on a work – the blasted stuff is there as plain as a pike-staff – the bugger of it is how to 'transubstantiate' these qualities into whatever medium one is using, whether paint or words or whatever.[8]

The artist does not impose what is not there; he sees what others do not. Jones's belief that an artist has to develop an acutely perceptive sensibility would underlie his saying to his psychotherapist in 1947, 'Don't make me normal.'[9]

Without a specially developed sensibility, even perfect mastery of technique produces valueless work. Technique or 'manual dexterity' is, Maritain writes, 'an abiding menace' (77) because it tends to displace sensitivity. Jones had realized this while in art school. As a conviction strengthened by Maritain, it helps to explain the primitive style of his small paintings and engravings at Ditchling and his subsequent stylistic transformations. He dreaded slick facility, and in his visual art would continually undo and counteract it.

An artist is a person transformed. According to Maritain, art demands 'that the whole appetitive faculty of the artist, his passions and his will, be orientated towards . . . Beauty' (71). This dedication precludes much else in life that is good: 'On the plane of his art, the artist is subject to a kind of asceticism, which may at times demand heroic sacrifice.' He makes no mention of sacrificing marriage, but Jones would later think himself obliged, as an artist, to forgo marriage because of the pressure to forsake or commercialize his art that a wife and family would involve. Maritain writes that the artist 'must be . . . perpetually on guard not only against the common-place allurement of facility and success, but against a crowd of subtler temptations and against the least slackening of his inward effort' and 'every loose activity' not involving artistic intensity. The artist 'must . . . of his own free will abandon fertile tracts for the arid and the perilous. . . . *in the order of making, and from the point of view of the beauty of the work*, he must be humble and magnanimous, prudent, upright, strong, temperate, simple, pure, ingenuous' (O'Connor's italics, 119–20). He must become a saint to his art. This is a way of putting what every artist knows, that art is not an activity but a life. It is, as Jones writes, 'totalitarian' in its demands.

Maritain repeats Aquinas on beauty, endorsing the three Thomistic conditions for its achievement that are familiar to readers of Joyce's *A Portrait of the Artist*. The first is integrity, which demands that art be objective in the sense described above. The second is proportion, order or unity – not an absolute but an inducement to the third condition, 'splendour' of form, or 'clarity' or 'radiance' of being (37), which is transcendent and is experienced in degrees ranging from pleasure to ecstasy.

Art is sacramental in its transcendent radiance or 'splendour of form' (*splendor formae* – Jones and Gill were both fond of this Thomistic expression). Neither Maritain nor Gill used the term 'sacrament' in this respect, but both emphasized that the splendour of art partakes of the splendour of God. In Maritain's words, 'every light' is an 'irradiation coming out of the primal clarity' (45). Beauty is therefore ultimately of God or, as Gill put it when discouraging realistic imitation, 'beauty is not achieved by making things like things, but by making things like God' (i.e., unified, radiant). 'Beauty, like Goodness & Truth is', as Gill liked saying, 'one of the names of God.'[10] Maritain claims that only such approximation of divine beauty can revive an exhausted art form. Although all this was new to Jones, he found it utterly convincing. In a draft of an essay written in 1943, he suggests that the ultimate disclosure of degrees of beauty will come at the end of time, when the angel Michael will shout, 'What is like God, in all this straw?' 'Then', Jones writes,

> we shall know how Chartres stands in relation to the Parthenon, the *Prima Vera* to Picasso's best, the lamp-shade in the room to the candelabrum of 1842, & see, strange enough, how Cannae stands to *blitzkrieg*, how Zama to the present Punic battle, simply as expressions of that 'virtue of the practical intellect' which the philosopher says art is

and defines as *recta ratio factibilium*, rational making.

All this implicitly supports a favourite contention of Gill, that making art is equivalent to praying. This notion would condition Jones's sense of his vocation and emerge as a theme in some of his later poetry. The identification of art with prayer healed, but only to a degree, an inner division between religion and art of which he had been aware since adolescence. He had felt that he was serving two masters – and serving art a good deal more than God. The unease this caused originated in his father's evangelicalism, which subordinated to religion all activities not excluded outright. Now he understood that art was 'good in itself', ratified and validated along with all things human and natural by Aristotelian metaphysics and by divine creation and the Incarnation. On this score, however, his thinking was not entirely reconciled with his feelings. For some years, at least, he would continue to wonder whether his total commitment to art was idolatrous, whether he was seeking 'that satisfaction in painting and engraving etc. that can only be found in God'.[11]

The relationship between art and God implied by beauty includes everything else. According to Maritain, all the beauty we see in nature (in landscapes, faces, bodies) has its 'sovereign analogue' in God, whose beauty is not relative or limited, but absolute and 'the wellspring of all beauty' (44-5). Sensitive appreciation is therefore, like artistic making, synonymous at some level with contemplative worship.

The relation between beauty and God profoundly moved Jones, who would, with close friends on various occasions, endorse what Maritain writes: 'every unison, or every harmony, every concord, every friend-ship and every union whatsoever between beings comes forth from the divine Beauty . . . which likens all things to one another, and calls them all unto itself' (45). In beauty, art – together with every other thing, including all relationships – has metaphysical significance. All are sacra-ments revealing God's presence. As a child, Jones had heard his mother ask her doctor, who was a Quaker, why Quakers have no sacraments. The doctor had replied, 'But Mrs. Jones, surely the whole of life is a sacrament.'[12] These words had impressed her son, who remembered them. Now he could see how, philosophically, they could be true.

The appropriate human response to beauty is love purified of concu-piscence or desire. According to Maritain, this is love of what the artist makes, which is, if he is a genius, '*a new analogue* of the beautiful'. It is also love of what in nature inspires this making, and love of God, to whom all analogues point (67). Jones and his companions often discussed love as determining the goodness of a work of art. They agreed that sentimentality was debased love; its effect on art, vulgarity.[13] Art can be 'Christian', Maritain writes, only if Christ is present in the artist 'through love' (101). In this respect, Christianity brings art 'closer to primitive art', giving 'what the artist needs most, simplicity, the peace of awe and of loving kindness, the innocence which makes matter docile and brotherly to man' (104). Jones responded warmly to this Franciscan aspect of Maritain's vision, which endorsed the love of particulars that would characterize his later work.

Judgement must guide love, however, for there are degrees of beauty, which exist, Maritain thought and Jones agreed, in a hierarchy of kinds. In 1930 Jones repeated in his own words in a conversation with a friend Maritain's assertion about these levels: 'to progress . . . is . . . to pass from the sensuous to the rational, and from the rational to the spiritual, and from the less spiritual to the more spiritual' (114).[14] In what amounts to a reversal of Freud, Maritain endorses Aquinas's borrowing from Aristotle: 'No one can live without delight. That is why he who is deprived of spiritual delights goes over to carnal delights' (114-15). (Jones marks with approval this passage in a copy of the book that he acquired in 1929.) Prayer and the sacraments are means to becoming more spiritually human, but so is art and the cultivation of aesthetic sensitivity. This is an inward, personal development, which Jones cultivated in himself. Maritain believed society as a whole capable of such development and of experiencing 'a second spring' – an image that he applied, as Jones also would, to the Middle Ages.[15] Jones believed in this positive social possibility and would write his later poetry in hopes of its eventually occurring, though not in his lifetime.

Anticipating Eliot's notion of dissociated sensibility, Maritain writes that the perception of art 'restores, for an instant, the peace and delectation at once of understanding and sense' (34) that characterized unfallen life in Eden. Expanding on this, Jones would assert that art escapes the effects of the fall because it achieves a unity and perfection absent in fallen nature. Years later, he would speak about this to friends, one of whom would remember, 'He talked about practically nothing else, in a sense.'[16]

From Maritain's neo-scholasticism, Jones took to heart certain formulations: 'we proceed from the known to the unknown' – words that a Dominican friend named John Baptist Reeves frequently repeated – and 'the virtue of *ars* is to judge.' These, he thought, expressed precisely what the artist does. 'For the "man on the job"', Jones wrote,

> there is no other way of proceeding – he has, with conscious deliberation, to 'judge', as the work proceeds, whether or not this line, mark, smudge, accent of colour, etc. (in the case of drawing) or this word, or order of words, this break of line, this space between lines, etc. (in the case of a writing) give those juxtapositions which best (in his judgement) create the forms which are most congruent and essential to the form and content of the whole, remembering that form and content must, by hook or by crook, be indissolubly wed otherwise there can be no whole.

Such judgement is practical, not ideological. However intellectually clarifying metaphysics might be, it had little bearing on practice. Jones wrote that he thought no

> amount of true philosophical or metaphysical definition will aid one bit, necessarily, the painting of a picture. The ability to paint a good picture does not come through philosophy or religion in any direct manner at all. They could only have indeed a damaging effect on the making of things if thought of as providing some theory to work by – a substitute for imagination and direct creativeness; and would so sadly defeat their own object – which is to protect the imagination from the slavery of false theory and to give the perfect law of liberty to our creativeness.[17]

He was convinced that Maritain's neo-Thomism served the only valid purpose of theory – to confirm creative liberty and protect it from false theory.

One of the convictions of Maritain, and also of Gill, is the 'unity of all made things'. Maritain stresses this continuity as including making 'from the art of the Shipbuilder to the art of the Grammarian and the Logician' (1). Jones would discover in Aquinas the underlying principle of this unity and would later write that all works of art and artefacture are the same 'in kind . . . once utility has to any degree been overpassed and . . . the quality of gratuitousness has to any degree been operative' [18] True to this principle of general unity, Gill wanted to abolish art-specialization. Let all men paint and sing and dance, he urged. Jones's belief in the unity of made things would encourage his writing poetry. In that poetry, Maritain's principle of 'the unity of all made things' would be the central theme of *The Anathemata* (1952). In it, made things exist in degrees of spiritual and aesthetic significance, which Jones calls, in his preface, a 'Jacob's ladder or song of degrees' (30). High on the ladder are the Venus of Willendorf, the Lascaux cave paintings, the Parthenon and Chartres cathedral. At the top is the Mass.

Maritain encouraged Jones in his remaining, in later years, a non-abstract artist even though Jones believed that all art was essentially abstract – a belief implicit in Post-Impressionist emphasis on artistic form. (He believed this early on. Gill was irritated by the term 'significant form' and used to ask. 'Significant of what?' but Jones thought the question 'never . . . quite fair' because a work of art had 'meaning' and 'life' deriving from a juxtaposition of forms.) Maritain stresses that the truth of art involves, or can involve, things outside itself. In a passage very important to Jones, Maritain writes that works of art reveal

> other things than themselves, that is to say as signs. And the thing signified may itself be a sign in turn, and the more the work of art is laden with significance (but spontaneous and intuitively grasped, not hieroglyphic significance), the vaster and the richer and the higher will be the possibility of joy and beauty. The beauty of a [non-abstract] picture or statue is thus incomparably richer than that of [purely abstract design in] a carpet . . . a Venetian glass, or . . . an amphora. (84)

From this passage Jones adopted the word 'sign', which he would use instead of 'symbol'. Here was reason to avoid pure abstraction in visual art: an attachment to the significance of created and man-made things. Since they are themselves 'signs', to exclude them would be to diminish the full potential of art for achieving or expressing significance. In the mid-1930s, when his friend Ben Nicholson insisted that all members of the Seven and Five Society, to which Jones belonged, make only abstract work, Jones did not conform and was voted out of the society.

Maritain's ideas lived in the continuing discussion which permeated Jones's life well into the 1930s and, intermittently, beyond. René Hague remembered that at Capel-y-ffin, where Jones visited the Gill family for months at a time from 1925 to 1927, Gill used *The Philosophy of Art*

> as a sort of text book on which he hung an exposition covering religion, social affairs, the arts, the whole of human life, which amounted to an education in a very special university. Night after night we studied [Hague, Jones, Donald Attwater and a Benedictine named Theodore Baily] under Eric's sort of presidency.

There were also what Hague called 'allied books', which included *Certainty* by Vivian Bickford, privately printed, in which 'the unity of indirect reference' is a criterion for discerning truth. This became, for Gill and Jones, an important concept by which many apparently unrelated things suggest an encompassing reality or meaning.[19] The concept was a way of seeing the world as an argument for Christianity. It also provided, for Jones, an aesthetic principle that justified Thomistic emphasis on analogy. Apparently unrelated things have associations and connotations that achieve an underlying unity. Much of his later poetry and painting achieves unity largely by 'indirect reference' and surprising analogy.

One of the participants in this ongoing conversation was, briefly, Jacques Maritain. In the spring of 1930, Maritain was in England, and on 20 March Gill recorded in his diary that he invited him to lunch with Jones and three other friends. One of these was Tom Burns, an editor for Sheed and Ward who had known Maritain and his circle in Paris in the early 1920s. Burns was the centre of a group that met to discuss life, morality, art and religion at his house in St Leonard's Terrace, Chelsea. The group included Jones; Christopher Dawson, the historian; Charles Burns, the psychiatrist brother of Tom; Martin D'Arcy, the Jesuit theologian; Donald Attwater, by now an expert in eastern Christianity; and Harman Grisewood, a broadcaster. They wanted to reform the Catholic Church in England, which they regarded as mindlessly conservative, parochially chauvinistic, and materialistic. They read and agreed with everything Maritain wrote. He was a model for them, for he had faced a similarly stultified Catholicism in France and was working to invigorate it. Burns had established a series of short books at Sheed and Ward called Essays in Order, with a wood-engraving of a unicorn by David Jones on the cover. The first of these books had been Maritain's

Religion and Culture (1929). When Maritain was in London again in 1932, Burns drove him to visit Gill who was then living at Pigotts in Buckinghamshire. Also in the car was Jones, who later remembered, 'Maritain & I carried on a conversation about the arts with Tom as interpreter.'[20] At one point, the car was stopped so that Maritain could relieve himself. Urinating by the side of the road, he said, 'You know our proverb? *Qui pisse contre vent mouille son pantalon.*' Afterwards, Jones and Burns used to quote the proverb to one other. In their efforts to invigorate and spiritualize the Catholic Church in England, they accepted that they were 'pissing against the wind' and would 'wet their pants'.

Having lost his original copy of *The Philosophy of Art*, Jones acquired a new copy in 1929. This survives, slightly marked and annotated. In the critical years leading up to the war, he saw political wisdom in the book, marking with approval Maritain's assertion that

> political and territorial nationalism is the natural safeguard of plain living and high thinking, and so of the very universality of intelligence and art; whereas another sort of nationalism, – metaphysical and religious nationalism, that which culminated in the Fichtean and Hegelian deification of the nation – does, by its efforts to enslave the understanding . . . to the physiology of a race or the interests of a state, jeopardise the existence of art and of every virtue of the mind. (113–14)

Cultural nationalism and regionalism provided material and motivation for art; political nationalism was important to Jones only to the extent that it preserved culture. In his preface to *The Anathemata*, he writes of cultural nationalism being subversive of political nationalism:

> Poetry is to be diagnosed as 'dangerous' because it evokes and recalls . . . something loved. In that sense it is inevitably 'propaganda', in that any real formal expression propagands the reality which caused those forms and their content to be . . . There is a sense in which *Barbara Allen* is many times more 'propagandist' than *Rule Britannia*. The more real the thing, the more it will confound their politics. (21–2)

As this suggests, Jones was not a political person, and of all Maritain's ideas, the aesthetic ones were most important to him. In the copy of Maritain's book acquired in 1929, he marks a passage in which Maritain sees Mary Magdalen's extravagant pouring of perfumes over the head and feet of Jesus as symbolic of the relationship of beauty to Christianity (117). In his own essays, Jones would refer to this scriptural episode, but interpret her act, and Jesus' defence of it, as validating gratuitous (non-utilitarian) symbolism as expressive of ultimate value. It made this Mary, for Jones,

> the mistress of all contemplatives and the tutelary figure of all that belongs to *poiesis*. The woman from Magdala in her golden hair wasting her own time and the party funds: an embarrassment if not a scandal. But an act which is of the very essence of *all* poetry and, by the same token, of any religion worth consideration.[21]

In his thinking, as expressed in his essays on culture, Jones was not subordinate to Maritain. He developed his own theory of art and culture, which he expressed most fully in his essays 'Art and Sacrament' and 'Use and Sign'. But Maritain's ideas were the foundation of all his thinking about art and culture, and his reliance on them never ceased. Because Maritain clarified for him what was right and true about art, Jones was clear about what might go wrong with art. In 1940, he feared that the modernist movement in literature would be wrecked by moralists, and he may have been largely right.[22] The moralists were Marxists and subsequently feminists and others concerned with art chiefly, if not solely, as it reflects and affects society – but their concern is not so much with society as with right and wrong. It is a concern that Maritain saw as essentially irrelevant to art. In the mid-1950s, Jones thought the principal danger to literature and art was subjectivity. He regretted the current adulation of 'subjective vision' by his friend 'dear Bertie' Read. 'At *bottom*', he thought, 'it's the trouble with Tom E[liot] also. In fact, in one form or another, it holds the field. At base, I suppose it is this subjectivism that separates them *all* from Joyce.' 'Not that one doubts what one is trying to do', he added, 'but it is a bit shaking when combined currents flow more & more against the kind of direction one feels to be the *only* direction that's worth while.'[23] When considering these things, he remembered Maritain. In 1955, he writes in 'Art and Sacrament':

> Round about 1923 there was available John O'Connor's translation of Maritain, and that, from the pen of a formal philosopher, provided certain reassurances and further data with regard to some matters which had occupied our thoughts as makers of things. It seemed to some of us at that period that important classifications made by Maritain (and some others) would have a correspondingly clarifying effect upon all subsequent discussion of the nature of Ars. In this we were over-optimistic. We did not sufficiently take into account the tide of subjectivism against which such objective views were struggling. (*EA*, 172)

Jones probably read most of Maritain's writings that were translated into English. At the time of his death, however, he possessed only a few.[24] One of these was *The Peasant of the Garonne* (London: Chapman, 1968), which I had sent, after visiting him, in 1971. I had given him to read a copy of the correspondence between Maritain and Marshall McLuhan, of whom he had not heard. After Jones's death in 1974, I saw again the book I had given him. He had read it. Maritain writes about 'the forms of enslavement which we owe to the empire of technique' as described by Jacques Ellul in *The Technological Society*, which Maritain had read and which had become a favourite book of Jones a few years earlier. In this passage Jones marks the words, 'Christianity . . . will . . . be the last resort of the human person and for those . . . who . . . will struggle to break from universal conditioning' (p.154).

For Jones, as for all modern writers and artists, there had been no living cultural tradition to provide clarity about art, its value relative to the rest of human experience and its ultimate significance. Maritain had retrieved and breathed life into an ancient tradition, providing Jones with a philosophy that armoured him against the theoretical and expressive fashions of the century that are, as formalists see it, inimical to art. Maritain helped him to achieve a confidence and direction that allowed him in making pictures and poetry, to transform the (in his words) acultural 'balls-up' into 'a kind of Praise' (*DGC*, 86). Whether or not this is the best art can do is a subject for endless debate between formalists and social moralists, but it was what Jones did. And those who value his work are indebted, as he was, to Jacques Maritain.

Notes

[1] David Jones, 'Life for Jim Ede', typscript, 5 September 1935. I am grateful to the trustees of the estate of David Jones for permission to quote from unpublished writing by Jones.

[2] Ernest Hawkins, interviewed 1 September 1987.

[3] Harman Grisewood, interviewed 19 June 1990, 5 October 1987.

[4] David Jones, letter to Tony Stoneburner, 30 August 1963.

[5] David Jones, letter to *The Times*, draft, 20 December 1945.

[6] *The Philosophy of Art* (Ditchling: St Dominic's Press, 1923), p.22. Page references appear hereafter in the text in parentheses.

[7] Eric Gill, *Art-Nonsense and Other Essays* (London: Cassell, 1929), p.52.

[8] David Jones, letter to Harman Grisewood, 22 May 1962.

[9] Harman Grisewood, interviewed 4 October 1987.

[10] Eric Gill, letter to G. Cary, 5 April 1934; Eric Gill, *Art-Nonsense*, p.58.

[11] David Jones, letter to Helen Ede, 13 August 1928.

[12] David Jones in conversation with Tony and Pat Stoneburner, written record, 9 June 1966.

[13] John Ginger, 'A Brother's Life: Reginald Lawson, 1981–1985', typescript.

[14] Harman Grisewood, interviewed August 1983.

[15] See *The Anathemata*, p.92.

[16] See David Jones, *Dai Greatcoat* (London: Faber, 1978), pp.134, 151, 156; Jim Ede, interviewed 31 May 1985.

[17] To Harman Grisewood, 22 May 1962; MS draft of incomplete, unpublished essay, *c.*1955; David Jones quoted by Ede, 'David Jones', *Horizon*, 8 (August 1943), 133.

[18] David Jones, *Epoch and Artist* (London: Faber, 1959), p.274.

[19] Donald Attwater, *A Cell of Good Living* (London: Chapman, 1969), p.97.

[20] To Tony Stoneburner, 12–16 August 1978.

[21] 'Use and Sign' (1962), *The Dying Gaul* (London: Faber, 1978), p.183.

[22] Letter to Harman Grisewood, 3 June 1940.

[23] Letters to Harman Grisewood, 10 January 1954, Tuesday, St Thomas Martyr, 1953.

[24] In addition to the book mentioned below, he had his own and Tom Burns's copy of *The Philosophy of Art* (1923), both acquired in 1929; *Some Reflections on Culture and Liberty* (Chicago: University of Chicago Press, 1933); *Art and Poetry* (London: Editions Poetry London, 1945), acquired at Christmas 1945; *Creative Intuition in Art and Poetry* (London: Harvill Press, 1954).

The Inscriptions of David Jones

EWAN CLAYTON

As a calligrapher and lettering artist, I wish to investigate the inscriptions of David Jones. I do not intend to present a comprehensive survey of his work,[1] rather I want to put together a few observations drawn from my own background as a maker of things.

The starting-point for what I have to say comes from a catalogue to an exhibition of sacred art at Lincoln in which the nun and art critic Sister Wendy Beckett wrote, 'many people are afraid of modern art, many people are afraid of contemplative prayer.'[2] With this arresting parallel she urges her readers to stay with the feelings that arise when they first face unfamiliar ground; even if those feelings are ones of uncertainty and confusion. It is not surprising that this suggestion comes from a nun for it is a contemplative approach. Her expectation is that if one stays in such a space, with an open mind, one will come to notice an inner dialogue developing, a frail and gentle structuring of thoughts and events like the bird's nest which, according to Irish legend, was built in St Kevin's hands when he stretched them out to pray.

It is this experience of looking that I wanted to bring to the inscriptions of Jones, and what follows is a partial account of the insights that arose. It is unapologetically subjective and follows three principal thoughts: that the inscriptions feel surprisingly familiar to me, that they have a strong physical presence, and that they evoke a ritual element.

Initially I approached the work expecting to face the mysterious, the enigmatic, the unknown, so my first reaction caught me completely by surprise: the inscriptions struck me as deeply familiar things. This feeling drew me back to my childhood, to two places that were important to me as I grew up, the island of Caldey and the village of Ditchling. I sensed that there were connections with these places in Jones's work.

My connection with Caldey is a family one. My grandfather and grandmother met and were married on the island. She, Celie McHardy, was the dairymaid there and he, Valentine KilBride, was a weaver.

Valentine, or Val as we called him, had been invited to the island by the abbot at the suggestion of Eric Gill. The monastery was looking for someone to weave up habit cloth for the monks. Val was a weaver waiting to occupy a workshop in the craft community at Ditchling which Gill had founded. Weaving up the habit cloth would take six months, exactly the time Val had to wait before he could occupy his workshop. It so happens that Jones visited the island at about the same time. Like Val, he knew the monastery well; they both took their meals in the monastic refectory. In the family we still have some of Val's photographs. One shows a painting, with inscriptions, which was on the refectory wall. It is by Dom Bede Bailey who had trained as an icon painter in the early twenties in Paris. He also lived at Capel-y-ffin with the Gill family for a short time. There is undoubtedly a similarity between this and Jones's first documented inscription: an inscription with a painting of a crucifix, made on the wall at Capel. I am certain that the work of Dom Bede Bailey, a monk from Caldey, must have been an influence here.

After my grandparents married they moved to Ditchling. In fact they moved into the very house, Woodbarton Cottage, where Jones had been living a year or so earlier. This cottage was the famous 'Sorrowful Mysteries', named, as my grandfather would later put it, after the woeful domestic arrangements of the three bachelors who had lived there. My aunt lives there to this day and in her kitchen there is another wall painting by Jones. It was painted directly on to the whitewashed brick one Palm Sunday in the early twenties.

At Ditchling Jones painted on many walls. It nearly determined the way he was remembered there. When there was a retrospective of his work at the Tate a few years ago, one of my aunts remarked with surprise: 'David Jones! Wasn't he the boy who used to paint on the walls?' The paintings that survive were painted on whitewashed bricks and wooden panelling.

The style of living at Ditchling was simple: little furniture, wood and brick floors, rush mats, whitewashed brick walls. No plaster, no electricity. The chapel is built in exactly the same style as the houses. Many walls also had stone inscriptions let into them. Sometimes they were memorials, more often they were roughly cut apprentice pieces from the stone carver's shop, unevenly spaced and brightly painted. In the early days of Ditchling it was frowned on to apply decoration to the walls. Decoration, it was thought, should be integral to the substance of things, part of the wall itself, not just a superficial application of ornament. Hence Jones's painting directly on to the walls and the use of inscriptions.

It is these rough, whitewashed, 'calcined' surfaces, these ordinary

stone carvings from the letterers' workshop, this light, this experience of
simple Christian community that I see as establishing the hinterland from
which Jones's use of inscriptions emerges. Perhaps this experience at
Ditchling is more formative than the earlier training in Trajan lettering
Jones had received at art school, an experience he found so disagreeable.
This experience is certainly prior to his later interest in late antique,
early Christian and classical vernacular lettering. It is these walls,
stones, whitewash, simple homes and workshops, this tradition of living
lettering at Ditchling which I believe marks the material substance of
Jones's work. It lies behind his slow searching through different techniques for preparing his surface and making his inscriptions until finally
he arrives at the chalked surface, so like the walls he knew at Ditchling,
Capel and Caldey.

All this means of course that I believe an understanding of the
Ditchling period is important to the making of Jones's inscriptions. I do
not see the process as one that started for him in the 1940s, as Gray
appears to suggest in her book. This commitment to inscriptions in the
1940s is new only in so far as it is a reawakening, a reaffirmation of this
area of work, the result of a new influx of meaning. Jones himself fully
indicates the importance of the Ditchling period in his letter to Gray on 4
April 1961, where he states that his inscriptions are a sequence stretching back to that time.

In the early days Jones worked in a number of materials: etching,
engraving and carving in wood and metals, painting on metals, wood and
whitewashed walls. As with any good arts and crafts letterer, his letter
forms respond to the materials and processes he uses. He makes many
forms of letters, engraved forms as in *The Town Child's Alphabet* and,
as in *Gulliver's Travels*, forms that clearly reflect the fact that they have
been cut from wood.

At times Jones's lettering may appear naive. He himself was apt to be
dismissive of his experience in the field, but he was an informed lettering artist. In addition to his Trajan studies at art school he had clearly
looked closely at the work of Eric Gill. There is an inscription on a
portrait of St Peter from 1922 (one of several similar portraits of saints
from about the same time) on which is a very carefully drawn piece of
lettering. The weighting, serifing, spacing and structure are all carefully
observed. He did learn what Gill could teach him (*pace* Nicolete Gray)
but significantly he elected to do something different. It is important to
recognize this because it emphasizes the true extent to which his work
was a matter of choice rather than accident.

Jones's inscriptions became popular and more widely known in the
1960s and 1970s. It was a time when making based upon experience,

transmitted tradition and convention was deeply unfashionable, within the narrow world of art education. Jones's supposed ignorance of 'correct forms' (no experienced letterer would think there were such things) was frankly played up by critics and art educationalists of the period. I view this as a misleading emphasis. Jones's lettering is far from a spontaneous experiment: it developed over a substantial period of time, through many influences, from an informed understanding of the detailed associations of historical forms. As René Hague writes:

> the remarkable thing about David's inscriptional work is that nothing is purely fanciful; every shape is determined by the particular evocation required in this place for this thought. There is nothing which makes the lettering of art nouveau and the nineties so foolish, nothing, on the other hand, standardised; there is no antiquarianism, but a great deal of scholarship, a knowledge of and contribution to tradition.[3]

I find myself in full agreement with these remarks.

You will remember that my point of departure for these fleeting thoughts was the surprising feeling of familiarity that I had felt towards Jones's inscriptions. My second impression of them was that they had a strong physical presence. I also felt that the physical relationship between the artist and his work intensifies as we move through the body of the inscriptions. This intensification struck me as a significant factor, I found it a clearer measure of the inscriptions' development, than tracking and describing Jones's changing use of letter shapes. This held little meaning for me.

Again this was a surprising discovery to make, especially for one who has taken a keen interest in historical traditions, as I have. And yet, perhaps, it is not so surprising. Though the story of lettering has, up to now, been written by those who trace history in terms of stylistic developments, in recent years there has been a detectable change in the way we look at this history. Stimulated by new technological developments in the field of electronic documents, we are realizing with some force that lettering always comes to us embodied in things. These things are wonderful and absorbing artefacts in their own right which enable us to transport, store, annotate and otherwise process letters. Through these things letters 'have substance and sure record' (*RQ*, 95). The physical is as important as the spiritual. They are two sides of the same coin. Making an inscription is an act of incarnation.

As Jones searches for the right physical surface, one that allows a making process – adding a bit here, taking away a bit there – there is a continuously more concentrated involvement with getting the physical

thing right until all aspects of the work surface, serifs, spaces come to
have an integrity in their own right. In earlier inscriptions like *O lux
Beatissima* (1946), the lines of lettering, though massed and brought
close to each other, are not adjusting to each other (this is especially true
of the serifs) as they will in later inscriptions. In *Optima Goreu Musa*
(1948) (fig. 7) there is an engagement with the surface; it is shaded and
scratched and lacerated, and from this lacerated surface letters emerge
into light. Now also the spaces between letters are being looked at, and
this begins to affect the shapes of the letters, particularly the serifing.
This is also true of an inscription like *Quia per Incarnati* where the
angle of serifs and their weight is being adjusted to balance with letters
above and below as well as on either side. In the major inscriptions of
the fifties such as *Cara Wallia Derelicta* (1959) (fig. 8) everything is
being adjusted to the way the eye can travel around the inscription as a
whole, the letters are being felt, smoothed, sorted out, made resonant

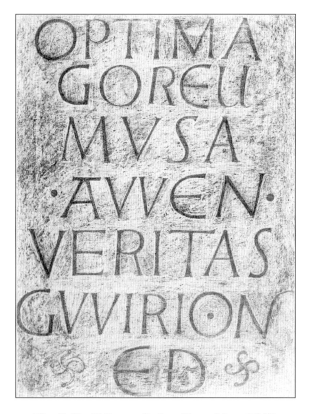

Fig. 7: David Jones, *Optima Goreu Musa* (1948)

Fig. 8: David Jones, *Cara Wallia Derelicta* (1959)

with each other, form and content coming together through minute adjustments.

In 'The Kensington Mass' Jones writes:

> Maura always says that. She always says after the incised inscriptions the portrait busts are where we are liveliest plastically. I'd rather overlooked the inscriptions – we were – aristocratic – there. It's an extremely interesting thing – one detects a streak of true refinement there – the spaces between the incisions have such significance in the best examples. Our masons seem to have a genuine understanding of the alphabet in a kind of physical way ... If 'and in them the word was made stone' is what posterity will say of us, it is some consolation. (*RQ*, 81)

This act of incarnation, an act of making real, is in Jones's theology a kind of Eucharist action; he could have been describing himself when he writes:

> in the prepared high room he implements inside time and late in time
> under forms indelibly marked by locale and incidence, deliberations
> made out of time, before all oreogenesis
>
> on this hill
>
> at a time's turn not on any hill
> but on this hill (*A*, 53).

These inscriptions are very particular things. Their particularity is demonstrated in every detail of the inscription he made in 1968 for Kathleen Raine: 'not one thing is insignificant.'[4]

I have followed up on two reactions to Jones's inscriptions, their familiarity and their physicality. My third and final reaction also came as a surprise and developed out of my reaction to the inscriptions' physical presence. I found I wanted to act them out. I sensed a ritual, a setting out of boundaries, a dedication of space, blessed, ratified, ascribed to. In reading the inscriptions I was reminded of ritual objects, a gospel book or missal. I wanted to proclaim them, to sing them, to mark them with gestures and crosses, to carry them solemnly from place to place, lay them out on the altar, to bend and whisper over them, to hold them up and proclaim them, to genuflect, hold a candle to them, intone:

> But first, careful that his right thumb is touching the letters of the writing,
> he must make the sign, down and across, beginning where the imposed,
> preclear-bright uncial reads, *Exiit edictum a Caesare Augusto*.

Just where, in a goodish light, you can figure-out the ghost-capitals.
And then he must (after he has joined his hands together) relate in a clear
high voice . . . (*A*, 219)

Of course this reaction should not be surprising; this is a genre of object
that any Roman Catholic, particularly of Jones's generation, would recognize. Altars and buildings abounded with inscriptions, from stations of the
cross, to altar cards, prayer cards, missals and lectionaries, psalters and
solemn gospel books with rubrics, directions and signs; their bars of plain
chant with square neums; their Latin and English combined. This is another
reason why his inscriptions are familiar. But it is interesting that these
inscriptions have a life of their own, they speak to us, and in the reading we
are seduced almost, to use the analogy made by the prophet Isaiah, into
being a participant, a minister of the word.

After I had written the last paragraph, I came across the following
reference: 'The inscriptions were important to David personally. He
used them as cards (like the mass cards on the altar) to help him through
his daily office as a Dominican tertiary.'[5]

I see these inscriptions as the core of Jones's work combining his
painterly eye and sense of occasion and language. I think they may be
his best work, at least his most complete expression of himself. I think
they should be central to any consideration of him as an artist and
maker. In them he collects himself up; all his considerations of cultural
history, the thread of the word, the particularities of place and time are
assembled into a disciplined expression of themselves that demand some
kind of enactment. Telling words.

I close with the final personal observation about Jones's work.
Whereas British calligraphy in the late twentieth century is not explicable
without the influence of Jones's inscriptions, his introduction of freer
arrangements of text, a new appreciation for the vernacular, my own
debt to him comes not from his letter shapes but through his poetry.
When I needed it, at a time when I had recently left a monastic life, I
found in his work an image that helped explain my essential fascination
as a calligrapher with the line.[6]

The images come from *In Parenthesis*, the long poem built upon his
experience of the First World War. Throughout *In Parenthesis* a soldier
is journeying towards the front line. What is that line? At one moment it
is the barrier between life and death, the border between the known
and the unknown, the edge, the *limes*, the frontier. This is the line all
letterers romance with; we approach it, run from it, sidle up to it, are
diverted from it; sometimes we seek to get beyond it.

In *In Parenthesis*, when the front line is reached, the line is shown to be unreal. It dissolves in an attack. Caught in the attack the artillery shells fall – felling Saxon and Celt, Gaul and German. And then through the wood where these men lie, twigs snapping, branches falling on all alike, steps the Queen of the Woods; this is her kingdom now. And just as Jones weaves the language out of allusions to the different cultures that have threaded their way through the wood, and makes something new of this space, so she also creates a greater whole in her tangled kingdom in which all are united (*IP*, 185–6). Yes, not one of these things have I lost, not one thing is insignificant. This is the kingdom where the line undoes itself into the general dance. This is the source which Meister Ekhart describes as the place where many images are engendered in one point. This is the line that the American Cistercian monk, Thomas Merton, had reached when, on meeting Kalung Rimpoche during his last trip to Asia, he said they recognized a sympathy between them, they knew they were both standing on the edge of something, waiting to go out and get lost in it. This is the point to which, under Jones's tutelage, I understand my art can lead me and essentially it is a mystical journey. And so we are back where I began ... 'many people are afraid of modern art, many people are afraid of contemplative prayer.' Ours is a journey not to be turned back from, a dance on the edge, a dance with the line,

> Come, Come, whoever you are,
> wanderer, worshipper, lover of learning,
> it doesn't matter.
> Even if you have broken your vow
> a thousand times, come.
> Come yet again, come![7]

Notes

[1]   See Nicolete Gray, *The Painted Inscriptions of David Jones* (London: Gordon Fraser, 1981), for a detailed survey of Jones's inscriptions.

[2]   Sr Wendy Beckett, *Sacred Art* (Lincoln: in catalogue 'The Journey', Usher Gallery, Lincoln, 1990), unpaginated.

[3]   René Hague, *David Jones* (Cardiff: University of Wales Press, 1975), p.68.

[4]   Gray, *Inscriptions*, p.93.

[5]   Jonah Jones, *The Gallipoli Diary* (Bridgend: Seren, 1989), p.92.

[6]   Bruce Harbert, 'The Quest for Melchisedek', *Clergy Review* (1990), 529–39.

[7]   Unascribed translation of a poem by Jelaludin Rumi (unpublished).

Doing and Making

A. C. EVERATT

I would like to suggest some parallels between David Jones's poetry and the moral philosophy of Alasdair MacIntyre. The comparative approach to Jones's poetry is not new: I think it is probably because he is so difficult to place that he invites this strategy. Comparisons with other poets like Blake, the Great War poets generally, Robert Graves, Eliot and Pound, John Cowper Powys, Basil Bunting and Geoffrey Hill have all been made. But there may also be something worthwhile in a comparison with the work of someone not a poet (or literary critic, or painter). It was in fact MacIntyre, not Jones, who was the starting-point for this exercise. MacIntyre's book *After Virtue* (1981)[1] is dominated by a calamity. At first the poems of Edwin Muir seemed to me to express a discontinuity that MacIntyre sought to express in morality. Muir's leaving the croft in Orkney for industrial Glasgow, the advent of atomic war, together with grave setbacks in his personal life, merge for him with a sense of a cosmic fall, after which the world is broken up into fragments. But as I thought more about the Break that MacIntyre describes and other features of his work, David Jones came to supplant Edwin Muir as the companion poet for the philosopher.

There are plainly predisposing similarities. Both MacIntyre and Jones acknowledge Maritain as a major influence. In *After Virtue* MacIntyre says he is his most important recent influence, and in later books that influence is apparent. In clarifying his ideas on art, Maritain is fundamentally important to Jones.

Aristotle is of major importance to MacIntyre, especially the *Nicomachean Ethics*; likewise, Jones says of a passage in that work, that without understanding it, readers will find his poetry incomprehensible.

Jones became a Roman Catholic in 1921, of a very settled kind. MacIntyre, having been brought up a Christian, tried at first to reconcile Marxism and Christianity and then came to think of Marxism as having displaced Christianity. The latter, he thought, lacked the resources to express the religious aspirations of modern man; it was untranslatable into modern social conditions. After adopting and abandoning many different political, religious and non-religious positions, MacIntyre in the mid-eighties became a Roman Catholic. He is a very restless thinker, but as far as I am aware, that is still his position. Again, the theme of 'unshared backgrounds' (a phrase of C. S. Lewis that Jones appreciated and pondered) has been a constant interest of MacIntyre.

There is no need to mention Jones's Celticism here: for MacIntyre, though in a less evident way, the Celtic inheritance and ways of life are vital. They have what seems to me to be a similar understanding of, pride in, and solidarity with displaced or defeated Celtic cultures; and an interest in the impact of empire on what used to be called primitive or less efficient societies. These obvious similarities suggest what might be a genuine concordance and mutual sympathy, and encourage one to go a bit deeper.

Jones was a maker of things, an artist, very self-consciously and deliberately an artist with a loyalty to fine art (different from his early mentor, Eric Gill), art to be practised and appraised by principles proper to it. MacIntyre, though a person of wide culture, nevertheless has restricted his written work to ethics (ethics, that is, understood in the old sense of including politics). The artist is not a doer, a moralist; the moralist is not an artist, a maker. The passage from the *Nicomachean Ethics* of which Maritain made so much and which Jones read in translation and discussed at length with his friends, and which is germane to MacIntyre's thought also, reads (in Thomson's translation) as follows:

> Among things liable to change we count (a) articles manufactured, (b) actions done. Making and doing are quite different activities. Consequently the rational faculty exercised in doing is quite distinct from that which is exercised in making. Moreover, they are mutually exclusive, for doing never takes the form of making, nor making of doing . . . An art is nothing more or less than a productive quality exercised in combination with true reason. The business of every art is to bring something into existence . . . and has its efficient cause in the maker and not in itself. This condition must be present, because the arts are not concerned with things that exist or come into existence from necessity or according to Nature, such things having their efficient cause in themselves. Then, since making is not the same as doing, it follows that art, being a kind of making, cannot be a kind of doing. We may even say that art and chance work in the same field.[2]

Jones follows through the implications of that in, amongst many other essays and poems, 'Art and Sacrament' (*EA*, 143–79).

We have then two considerable intellects, united in sympathies and subject to similar influences, and I would have thought seeing themselves as part of a common tradition, yet each exercising his skills, deliberately excluding the subject matter, or modalities of the subject matter, of the other. So it is interesting to recognize the same concepts and sometimes meandering trains of thought and obstacles and commitments appearing in the work of each, and with, I trust, some mutual illumination.

MacIntyre was born in 1929, read Classics at Queen Mary College, London, and then philosophy at Manchester, under Dorothy Emmet. An early interest was Hegel (he later co-edited a volume of essays on Hegel). Of his first book *Marxism and Christianity*, initially published in 1953 when he was twenty-three, he writes in the 1968 preface:

> Then I aspired to be both a Christian and a Marxist, or at least as much of each as was compatible with allegiance to the other and with a doubting turn of mind; now I am sceptical of both, although also believing that one cannot entirely discard either without discarding truths not otherwise available.[3]

Chapter 1 has as its motto Spengler's aphorism 'Christianity is the grandmother of Bolshevism.' Interestingly, in an essay on Spengler's *Decline of the West*, Roger Scruton asserts that Spengler's account of the Enlightenment and its successors is intellectual history at its best, that 'Spengler reminds us that, precisely because morality had become a problem for us, something vital to human happiness has been lost. In one lucid paragraph he conveys a thought that occupies MacIntyre through a whole book of hesitations.'[4] He was professor of sociology at Essex in the late sixties, round about the time of the student disturbances. It was his belief then that the historical phase and social conditions entered intimately into any adequate account of human action and reasoning about justice and any kind of moral belief. His very popular *A Short History of Ethics*[5] appeared in 1967, and is still in print and used by students – though by the 1980s he realized it was not in fact possible to write such a book. There was no standpoint, he had to concede, from which one can evaluate the values and distinctive moral reasoning of different cultures – there was diversity, but no unity. After moving to the United States, in 1981 he published the well-known and disturbing book already mentioned, *After Virtue*, which now forms the first volume of a trilogy, the others being *Whose Justice? Which Rationality?* (1988) and *Three Rival Versions of Moral Enquiry* (1990). *After Virtue* signals his disenchantment with Marxism, which disappears altogether from the next two volumes, and with it comes the deepest cultural pessimism. The last paragraph reads:

> It is always dangerous to draw too precise parallels between one historical period and another, and among the most misleading of such parallels are those which have been drawn between our own age in Europe and North America and the epoch in which the Roman Empire declined into the Dark Ages. Nonetheless, certain parallels there are. A crucial turning point in that earlier history occurred when men and women of goodwill turned aside from the task of shoring up the Roman imperium and ceased to indentify the continuation of civility and moral community with the maintenance of that imperium. What they set themselves to achieve instead – often not recognising fully what they were doing – was the construction of new forms of community within which the moral life could be sustained so that both morality and civility might survive the coming ages of barbarism and darkness. If my account of our moral condition is correct, we ought also to conclude that for some time now we too have reached that turning point. What matters at this stage is the construction of local forms of community within which civility and the intellectual and moral life can be sustained through the new dark ages which are already upon us. And if the tradition of the virtues was able to survive the horrors of the last dark ages, we are not entirely without grounds for hope. This time however the barbarians are not waiting beyond the frontiers; they have already been governing us for some time. And it is our lack of consciousness of this that constitutes part of our predicament. We are waiting not for a Godot, but for another – doubtless very different – St Benedict. (*AV*, 263)

He could have been glossing the crisis of Empire in Jones's 'The Tribune's Visitation' and echoing the prayers in 'The Tutelar of the Place'.

The following two volumes narrate the histories of Augustinianism, Aristotelianism, Thomism and the Scottish Enlightenment and Hume; and the clash between the Enlightenment and its derivatives (the precursor of modernism), the Nietzschean genealogy of the will (the precursor of postmodernism), and neo-Thomism. Though the difficulties are immense in judging between traditions (there being no independent position, no neutral standpoint), nevertheless it has to be done. This is his concern in these volumes. They *are* full of hesitations, but he comes to the conclusion that the Thomist tradition is 'the best so far' and so (provisionally) he adopts it.

I want to sketch now, very briefly, some similarities and differences in MacIntyre's ethics and Jones's poetic vision, under three headings: the Break, stories and tradition.

Fundamental to all of MacIntyre's later work, is the idea of a gross and irreversible break in the intellectual and moral history of the West. Archaic and classical antiquity, the so-called Dark Ages and Middle Ages and early Renaissance all shared (though in different ways) an idea of human nature intelligible to reason. A human action is intelligible as rational deliberation about means to an end, itself understood and set by reason. To present an action compelling understanding and assent, it must stand to reason (about which the third witch in 'Mabinog's Liturgy' in *The Anathemata* is also insistent). The shared assumptions about human nature and the intelligibility of human action which upheld what he calls classical morality disappeared in the seventeenth century. This was the great crisis of early modernity which the Enlightenment project sought to overcome by attempting to construct a new morality: universal in application, free of religious presuppositions and scientific in temper. The subsequent history of this project has shown that each new theory of ethics proposed in turn by Hume, Diderot, Kant, Kierkegaard and the Bloomsbury Group has displaced its predecessor, not improved it, and the upshot (to cut a long and interesting story short) is a society where moral choices boil down to individual preferences, and where ethical discourse is incorrigibly disordered. The significance of moral terms was given by social context and assumptions about human nature and human action; when these disappeared, moral terms were left without a stable sense, reference and context. Now ineffective moral discourse goes on and on and on, without a hope of reaching a conclusion. Now there is so little common ground, we can no longer even disagree about morality. Fragments of the old morality remained; you find them, he says, in Jane Austen (*AV*, 181–7 and 239–43) and William Cobbett (*AV*, 238–9 and 243), but they are fragments indeed. The outcome for the modern world is that an adequate moral language has been invalidated by the passage of time, rather than by disproof. Defeated, but not refuted, but defeated none the less. 'We operate in a terrain overrun by the enemy' (*EA*, 106).

Jones has a similar tale to tell about the invalidation of signs and images. The Break becomes apparent during the Great War; an age ended at the Battle of the Somme. But this had been anticipated in the nineteenth century when a kind of Rubicon had been crossed. The signifying materials to hand for the artist had changed utterly. The sense, reference and context of candles and swords, priests and bards, horses and birds, which had had a more or less unbroken history stretching far back, were now dysfunctional. That wood should cease to evoke the central event in human history was for Jones the loss of a world. The timber of the boatyard, the mast and keel of a ship, the material of sculpture and carving, the dark wood where so many lost their way, and the forest where the maimed king was entangled, the plantation where the enemy front-fighters were entrenched, the domain of the Queen of the Woods, and the fuel for shivering infantrymen were mutually enriching analogues of sign and image and matter. Indeed, he tells us, the very search for waste timber for a comforting fire led him to the sight of the re-enactment of Calvary, to the holy rood and rootless tree, whose scales measure the compensation for the fall. This, and a host of images and signs, were invalidated, persisting here and there in fragments, but on the whole, done with. To live in this new world with a memory of the old not shared by others is a strange business – we operate in a terrain occupied by strangers.

Let us move on from this calamitous interruption – while we remember the wounded king but still await the hero, or shift uncomfortably among the ruins of morality – to the importance of story.

MacIntyre lives in a story-shaped universe. In being born we are all plunged into a story; we are all born with a past. We are all set a task. Events are intelligible only as actions – what people do to bring about something good. Actions acquire significance, come into their own, only as parts of a story. Behaviourism and determinism have no stories to tell. We have goals, but goals set in an unpredictable future. We arrange our intelligible universes and conceptual schemes through stories.

> I can only answer the question 'What am I to do?' if I can answer the prior question 'Of what story or stories do I find myself a part?' We enter human society, that is, with one or more imputed characters – roles into which we have been drafted – and we have to learn what they are in order to be able to understand how others respond to us and how our responses to them are apt to be construed. It is through hearing stories about wicked stepmothers, lost children, good but misguided kings, wolves that suckle twin boys, youngest sons who receive no inheritance but must make their own way in the world and eldest sons who waste their inheritance in riotous living and go into exile and live with the swine, that children both learn and mislearn both what a child is and what a parent is, what the cast of characters may be in the drama into which they have been born and what the ways of the world are. Deprive children of stories and you leave them unscripted, anxious stutterers in their actions as in their words. Hence there is no way to give us an understanding of any society, including our own, except through the stock of stories which constitute its initial dramatic resources. Mythology, in its original sense, is at the heart of things. (*AV*, 216)

The myths that carried the gospel truths and recollections of war were mostly stories of Arthur and legends from the *Mabinogion*. They were a good fit: task-set heroes on other-world quests, war-bands led by a damaged king, rearguard actions, the subjugation of the real Britons of these islands, their persistence in defeat. The repertoire is rich enough to supply archetypes to unify all individual lives. MacIntyre asks:

'In what does unity in an individual life consist?' The answer is that its unity is the unity of a narrative embodied in a single life. To ask 'What is the good for me?' is to ask how best I might live out that unity and bring it to completion. To ask 'What is the good for man?' is to ask what all answers to the former questions have in common. But now it is important to emphasise that it is the systematic asking of these two questions and the attempt to answer them in deed as well as in word which provides the moral life with its unity. The unity of a human life is the unity of a narrative quest. Quests sometimes fail, are frustrated, abandoned or dissipated into distractions; and human lives may in all these ways also fail. But the only criteria for success or failure in a human life as a whole are the criteria of success or failure in a narrated or to-be-narrated quest. (*AV*, 218)

It was in pondering these reflections of MacIntyre on the quest as definitive of the unity of human life (without which he says there is no personal identity), set down without any reference to Jones, that I have come a little closer to understanding the role of quest and question in *The Anathemata*, where it is so dominant, and that I find it can be supported by a systematic ethics which, for his artistic purposes, he has consciously disregarded. The ideal moral agent in Aristotle is the good citizen – magnanimous and full of good sense, playing a part in the life of the city. In Aquinas, MacIntyre sees the ideal moral agent as the enquirer, the wayfarer, *homo viator* – the questing voyager. In *After Virtue*, he says:

We have then arrived at a provisional conclusion about the good life for man: the good life for man is the life spent seeking the good life for man, and the virtues necessary for the seeking are those which will enable us to understand what more and what else life for man is. (*AV*, 219)

You have to weigh anchor and make for the open sea.

Jones had many heart-searchings about the use of myths and the way they get confused with truths, but he trusted his instincts that they enable truths to be told and to present, in *The Anathemata*, the central truth of life – the story of a victim who restores order, voyaging from one world to another, in which all participate partly or fully, making of all individual quests one voyage.

Tradition emerges as the dominating concept in MacIntyre's later work – the way traditions begin, are threatened, flourish, merge, overcome crises, can and cannot be appraised; what it means to belong to a tradition. The tradition in which MacIntyre feels at home is the tradition of tradition. He defines a tradition as 'an argument extended through time'.[6] Traditions are usually inaugurated by a text, very probably sacred; they come to be questioned and demand a response. 'Traditions, when vital, embody continuities of conflict' (*AV*, 222), they have their distinctive and respective skills of reasoning; they recognize masters and authorities within the tradition; good masters enable their pupils and apprentices to go beyond them. 'An adequate sense of tradition manifests itself in a grasp of those future possibilities which the past has made available to the present' (*AV*, 223); good traditions make progress, they are incremental. The good tradition especially has a capacity to overcome what he calls an epistemological crisis; it has resources to recover, reset goals, and still remain true to type. A tradition has its own table of virtues and own distinctive practices. A practice is a notion in MacIntyre that has attracted a lot of critical attention. It is, I believe, pretty exactly what Jones means by *disciplina* – he usually uses the Latin term. Traditions support institutions. A good tradition is rational and dialectical. MacIntyre maintains that Edmund Burke 'contrasts tradition with reason and the stability of tradition with conflict. Both contrasts obfuscate ... When tradition becomes Burkean, it is always dying or dead' (*AV*, 221). These are, if you like, the formal properties of tradition – the necessary conditions a way of life must satisfy to be a tradition.

When we come to those particular ways of life and cultural sequences which he admires as traditions, they are the societies and communities of American Indians, Scottish crofters, Gaelic Irish, South Sea Islanders; or the great synthesis of Presbyterian religion, Roman-Dutch law and the universities of seventeenth-century Scotland, which Hume subverted: once flourishing communities, now colonized underdogs, victims of empire – communities we recognize in Jones as despoiled by the Ram. They are communities where the balance between town and country was still preserved, as in Spengler's first two culture phases. And there is the most important intellectual and moral tradition continuous from pagan antiquity to Christian early modernity, which thinks well of both the hero and the saint, both honour and virtue, and is now in fragments.

There is a kind of rhythm in Jones, different from the rhythm of tradition in MacIntyre, of proposition and refutation, thesis and antithesis. The dialectic of *The Anathemata* is of open question and hidden answer, the quest itself being the answer. But there is also something else. One can extend Thomas Dilworth's idea that the poem is a displaced epic to understand the idiom of the poem as displaced prophecy. Prophecy, according to St Thomas Aquinas, is made up of two parts – the *cognitio prophetica* and the *denuntiatio*: the seeing into the heart of things, reading the signs of the times, the function of the seer; and the condemnation, or warning, to the people. The denunciation is hidden in the question. If the question is not asked, the household and community are in thrall to blind fate. The great questioning epic of *The Anathemata* is anticipated in part in *In Parenthesis*:

> You ought to ask: Why,
> what is this,
> what's the meaning of this.
> Because you don't ask,
> although the spear-shaft
> drips,
> there's neither steading – not a roof-tree. (*IP*, 84)

If the prophetic question is asked, and answered by the undertaken quest, 'the King would have been restored to his health and his dominion in peace' (*IP*, M, 210).

The discrepancy between argument and enquiry may not go all that deep. Other features of tradition are interestingly concordant. Like MacIntyre, Jones is very sensitive to the critical balance between city and country; there is the same allegiance to the traditions of the dispossessed and defeated people; the continuum and integrity of pagan and Christian – Virgil, as well as Isaiah, heralds the Incarnation; the presence within a tradition of different crafts and perspectives, but nevertheless bound by common ties. The hall priest in 'The Sleeping Lord', musing about past rulers of the land, before saying Grace, refers affectionately to this disparity of practice:

Some but recent, others far, far, far back: such as Belinos of whom the Bard of the Household claimed to have some arcane tradition. About which, he, himself, the Priest of the Household, thought of uncertain authenticity; but, to say the truth, he was dubious of much that these poets asserted though they were indeed most skilled artists and remembrancers and conservators of the things of the Island, yet he suspected that they tended to be weavers also of the fabulous and were men over-jealous of their status and secretive touching their *traditio*, but then, after all, their *disciplina* was other than his and this he knew for certain that whatever else they were, they were men who loved the things of the Island, and so did he. (*SL*, 82)

In fact, the whole of the hall priest's soliloquy is a beautiful gathering together of the strands of a tradition.

There are complexities and paradoxes in Jones's feeling for tradition at which I have scarcely glanced. In 'The Book of Balaam's Ass', for instance, he has to confront the thought that the great European tradition, in which he was a participant, had culminated in massive slaughter on the Western Front. He had, moreover, affection and respect for those Roman soldiers, the *centuriones*. These were men having authority, and imperial authority has its down side, but they were part of his tradition, none the less. I trust, however, that the correspondence I have suggested in these matters, sketchy though it must be, can be seen to emerge as a structuring element in the mentality and sensibility of both David Jones and Alasdair MacIntyre, and casts light on each.

Notes

[1] Alasdair MacIntyre, *After Virtue* (London: Duckworth, 1981), see especially pp.1–5. From here on, when referred to in the text, this work will appear as *AV*.

[2] J. A. K. Thomson, *The Ethics of Aristotle* (London: Penguin, 1953), bk 6, ch.4, pp.175–6.

[3] Alasdair MacIntyre, *Marxism and Christianity* (London: Duckworth, 1953), p. vii.

[4] Roger Scruton, *The Philosopher on Dover Beach* (Manchester: Carcanet, 1990), p.6.

[5] Alasdair MacIntyre, *A Short History of Ethics* (London: Routledge & Kegan Paul, 1967).

[6] Alasdair MacIntyre, *Whose Justice? Which Rationality?* (London: Duckworth, 1988), p.12.

On Not Knowing Welsh:
David Jones and the Matter of Wales

A. M. ALLCHIN

I want in this essay to look at two things which, in David Jones's mind, were closely connected. First, and briefly, I want to consider his view of the sacramental quality of the whole world, a sacramentality which he saw focused in the mystery of Christ made present in the celebration of the Eucharist. Then I want to look, in a little more detail, at some of the aspects of his concern for the tradition of Wales, and in particular for the words of the Welsh language. It is, of course, always said that he did not know Welsh. He said it insistently himself, and we must accept what he says. We shall, however, need to recognize that there is a variety of ways of not knowing Welsh, his way differing considerably from that of most of his non-Welsh-speaking fellow countrymen, whether in England or in Wales.

First, on the question of the sacraments: David Jones once told me of an incident in his childhood, which seems to me in its own way almost as prophetic for his later life as the better-known incident in which he described how he got out of bed to see the mounted soldiers riding by on a recruiting exercise in the first months of the South African war. The other incident is one to which Tom Dilworth refers in his contribution to this collection of essays. I was never able to suppose that Jones had not spoken of it to others; certainly it had remained very vivid in his memory.

The occasion was a visit from the family doctor, who happened to be a Quaker and who had come to see Jones's elder sister who was in bed with some illness. As Jones's mother was seeing the doctor out at the end of the visit, with her son, perhaps six or seven years old, standing at her side, Mrs Jones said, 'But what I can never understand, doctor, is how you Quakers manage without the sacraments.' The doctor replied 'But Mrs. Jones, don't you know that everything is a sacrament.' They were words on which Jones was to meditate for the rest of his life.

There is much that could be said about this fragment of conversation. It suggests a mutual confidence and understanding between the mother and the doctor, a willingness to entrust one another with deeply felt convictions, which speaks well of both of them. It also suggests that Jones's mother had a distinctly more catholic and sacramental approach to religion than his strongly evangelical father. This is a small point, but one which deserves more attention. It may be that one of the early sources of Jones's sacramental view of reality lay in the often unspoken attitudes and beliefs of his mother. There are other places where it is clear that from early childhood Jones was made aware of differences within the Christian world as between Catholic and Protestant. There was a figure called Dr Pusey who seemed to be a cause of dispute. Here again were matters which were to be with him throughout his life.

I turn now to the question of Jones's knowledge of Welsh. Let us start from Saunders Lewis's clear declaration: 'It is a grief for David Jones that he has no Welsh.' Of course, Lewis goes on to say that he makes the utmost use of translations and that he corresponds with scholars who are experts. But he himself 'has no Welsh'.

One is inclined almost at once to dissent from this statement. The use of Welsh words in Jones's writing and the use of Welsh in his inscriptions is consistently accurate and well judged. It certainly suggests that somehow or other Jones acquired at least some knowledge of the words of the Welsh language. Doubtless he was helped very much by his friends in the choice of passages for incorporation into his inscriptions, above all by Saunders Lewis. But not all the help of others could have dispensed him from the necessity of himself feeling his way into the words of which he would make use. He certainly seems to have had that inward feeling for the words incorporated in, for example, the great *Cara Wallia Derelicta* (fig. 8) inscription.

It is indeed clear that although he never learned to read Welsh fluently, let alone to speak it or understand it when spoken, Jones was not without a knowledge of, and a feel for, the language. Here he is, in July 1935, staying at Skipton with the Christopher Dawsons, writing a letter to René Hague.

Late after lunch July 3rd. Went for a walk over the hills alone this morning and back under deep green places by the river and sat and shouted psalms in Welsh. I've got a Book of Common Prayer which gives me great pleasure and you can learn a few words as you go along. Don't you think the sound of the words for Blessed V. Mary good – they are *Fendigedig Fair Forwyn*, pronounced roughly Vendigedig Vire (like i in fire) Vorwein. (*DGC*, 74)

For once Jones did not get the pronunciation altogether right: Vorwin not Vorwein.

Jones's interest was principally in the old Welsh of the Middle Ages and the classical Welsh of the period of the Bible and the Book of Common Prayer. But he was not altogether ignorant of more current forms of the language. Here is a quotation from another letter to René Hague written almost thirty years after the passage just quoted:

Strange thing, I was tearing up masses of stuff and my eye caught a glimpse of a Feb. (1964) issue of the Radio Times (Welsh Home Service Edition) of a girl's face and I thought Lord! that's quite like darling Valerie – suppose its a south-Welsh type – and then I drew out the paper and it jolly well was Valerie in a Welsh-language television play, looking a bit different because of television make up of course. Then I did my best to read what it said and after a little bit about the play it said *Merch amryddawn yw Valerie Price sy'n chwarae rhan Tessa* – Girl versatile is V.P. who plays the part of Tessa. *Magwyd hi yng Nghwmllynfell ac ymhlith pethau eraill bu'n ffisiotherapydd, athrawes, model a phencampreg hyrdlo Cymru.* Nurtured (was) she in Cwmllynfell and among many other things has been a physiotherapist, a (school) teacher, a model, and champion hurdler of Wales. Well, it's the last bit that amuses me, I had never heard of her prowess as a hurdler ... I knew about the other occupations – *ffisiotherapydd* is jolly nice isn't it, for physiotherapist. (*DGC*, 197)[1]

Of course it is not much being able to make out an item in the Welsh section of the *Radio Times*, though it is better than nothing. Aneirin Talfan Davies put the matter more exactly than most when he wrote: 'He was profoundly frustrated by the fact that he could not read Welsh easily.' Grammar, syntax, the conjugations of the verbs, these things defeated him. But the words of Welsh he loved and savoured.

I should like to illustrate this knowledge of Welsh words, leading to a delighted appreciation of their meaning and flavour, by quoting some extracts from letters which Jones wrote to me in the years between 1967 and 1972.

I first wrote to him in August 1967, sending a copy of the periodical *Sobornost* which contained an English translation of Saunders Lewis's lecture on Ann Griffiths given at the National Eisteddfod in Newtown in 1965,[2] and I first went to see him soon afterwards.[3] The lecture was by all accounts a very memorable occasion. Poems were written about it both in English and in Welsh. It was one of the key moments when in later life, as a Roman Catholic, Saunders Lewis reclaimed something at the heart of his earlier inheritance as a Calvinistic Methodist.

Jones writes:

Yes, I am most pleased to have the address that Saunders L. gave in 1965 when the Eisteddfod Genedlaethol was at Y Drenewydd. I am a member of the *Cymmrodorion Society*, so receive the Transactions but can't recall Saunders' address appearing in them – but even had I seen it I should not, alas, have been able to read it because of my terribly scanty, almost non-existent, knowledge of *yr hen iaith*, so the translation in *Sobornost* is most welcome to me.

David Jones was greatly struck by the emphasis on the incarnation which characterizes Ann Griffiths's hymns and letters, and which was brought out in Lewis's lecture, and also in the accompanying article by H. A. Hodges, who had made the translation. To Jones it would have seemed more probable that the Calvinistic Methodist movement, of which Griffiths was a part, would have produced a contemplative 'who had as her inscape, as it were, the Passion':

I have of course heard about Ann Griffiths from various Welsh friends but it takes a person such as Saunders to really make plain, in his inimitable way, her real significance – the extraordinary phenomenon she presents suddenly appearing within the most unlikely religious milieu of late 18th cent. Calvinistic Wales.

Then in a note in the margin he adds, 'I should rather *expected* [*sic*] there to have been more than one Welsh Catherine Emmerich.'

This led him to the memory of a sermon heard in his childhood which linked him directly to the faith and devotion of evangelical Wales:

I myself have heard in my childhood, a clergyman, a Welsh speaking friend of my father's, preach a sermon in English on a Good Friday that had very considerable evocative concentration on the Instruments of the Passion and moreover he did not fail to connect the Immolation on the Tree with the Oblation at the Supper, though he was *decidedly* Protestant theologically. But though this was over sixty years ago I can still hear him say with a *very* Welsh inflection, 'He *drank* the Cup'.

In Welsh Nonconformity, the approach by way of the doctrine of the atonement did not necessarily exclude a recognition of the central place of the sacrament, to which Jones was to give so much attention. Indeed, had he known more of the importance of the sacrament of Communion in early Methodism, he would have found surprising cross-references from the one tradition to the other.

In a letter written a few days later he comments further on the life and circumstances of Ann Griffiths:

It has occurred to me while reading Saunders' thing that if Dolwar means what, in my amateur and guesswork fashion I take it might mean, viz. *dol*, a meadow and *gwar*, 'mild', 'gentle', 'pure', 'pleasant' (it appears to equate with *tirion* and other words more or less indicative of pleasantness) then it is a rather appropriate site name for Ann's habitation. Still more when the parish or locality chanced to be Llanfihangel-yng-Ngwynfa, for is not *gwynfa* one of the Welsh terms for paradise? It merely struck me as a remarkable coincidence, – that's all, – that is unless my etymology (a dangerous matter to meddle in, without proper foundation) is all astray.

It seems as if on this occasion Jones's etymology has gone astray. While the word *dol* certainly means meadow, the word *gwar* also means nape of the neck, ridge, margin; and this seems the more likely origin of the second part of the name. What intrigued and indeed amused Jones was that in his understanding the name of both the house and the village seemed almost excessively appropriate to the character of the person who lived there:

But it struck me that supposing we were dealing with some figure about whom legend had clustered who lived a millennium and a half back, in say the 'The Age of the Saints' in 6th cent. Wales, instead of a figure of only a century and a half back, then I can imagine the learned might well tend to suspect these site – and locality – names as – what's the term they use? – 'onomastic' (?) juggling by hagiographical writers, 'In that dear middle-age these noodles praise', to accommodate the site-names with the character of the person associated with those sites.

In a letter written on Ash Wednesday, 28 February 1968, Jones comments on some of the problems involved in the translation of liturgical texts. This was a subject on which he felt very strongly, indeed almost despairingly since the reforms initiated by Vatican II seemed to him monstrously wrong-headed:

Remembering that you noted my faintly delineated *Hora novissima tempora pessima sunt: vigilemus* you may be pleased to hear that above that large inscription in a frame (with a couple of lines from Gruffydd Gryd's [*sic*] poem in Welsh and Latin about 'Who is the man who owns the Crown' and that superb piling up of words and actions in the Canon: hostiam + puram, hostiam + sanctam, hostiam + immaculatam – the solemnity and potent weight of which is reduced to this 'Holy and perfect sacrifice' in the new English version of the Canon – and there is the loss of the manual *signa* – underneath) I have put under a reproduction of a very early painting of the Deipara (6th cent. in church of S. Maria Nuova) a little inscription in red which I found I'd made on a bit of torn paper and re-found in the general

chaos of my stuff, which reads: *MAM HAWDDGAR* the Welsh equivalent to
MATER AMABILIS a case where in English the usual translation 'Mother
most amiable' chaps find so unidiomatic, whereas *hawddgar chances* to be
perfect in Welsh with all kinds of undertones and overtones and is good
idiomatically (I'm told) and certainly is very beautiful phonetically, – interesting how very chancy it all is – I mean what happens in one language or
another . . .

Then there follows one of those ample Jones marginal notes, this time in
green biro:

It also happens that in the words *praeclarum Calicem* the English transla-
tors appear not to have been able, I think it is a case of not *can't* but don't
want to! – to find an equivalent to *praeclarum* and have simply left a blank
and translate *Calicem* (cup) whereas it translates *Caregl rhagorol* in Welsh
and *rhagorol* equates extremely well with *praeclarum* for it means excellent, excelling, splendid in its pre-eminence, in fact the element *rhag* –
means 'pre-' 'fore'. And it chances that just as the Romans addressed
certain chaps as *Clarissmus* so the term *rhaglaw* was used in Welsh of
highly placed men. Pilate was *rhaglaw* of Judea and I *think* is so termed in
Luke III – yes, he is – '*a Phontius Pilat yn rhaglaw Judea*'.

In this letter we see Jones at work, in the amazing clutter of his room,
in the private hotel in Northwick Park Road, with the inscriptions great
and small, Latin, Welsh and English, stacked up around the walls, and
with his copy of the Missal and the Bible in Welsh close at hand in order
to check the details of what he wanted to say. We see his dismay at the
tendencies to simplify and secularize which he perceived in the reforms
going on in his church. We see his delight in the traditional language of
the eucharistic prayer both in Latin and in Welsh. Although he would
hardly be pleased that the current Welsh translation of the Canon of the
Mass has turned to the word *cwpan*, at least he would be glad that the
word *rhagorol* remains, *cwpan rhagorol*.

At this point there comes in his letter another marginal note, this time
in red. 'Sorry about all this stuff. Sounds as if I knew these languages,
which I do not. But I'm intrigued with what is possible and works in one
language and not at all in another.'

In a talk given on the Welsh Home Service in April 1959, Jones
declared: 'I would end rather with a confession; it so happens that I am,
by this chance or that, mixed up with, involved in, or at least I wonder
about, three things, the arts which I try to practise, the tradition of the
Cymry, and the continuance of any sort of sacramental religion.' All
these things he felt to be threatened by the developing technology which

he believed more and more cut off the present from the past, and dimin-
ished our sense of our true humanity.

We have looked then, in this discussion, briefly at Jones's lifelong
concern to understand the sacramental quality of all life; something he
believed was established and made firm in the sacramental givenness of
the mystery of Christ. We have also considered his lifelong desire to
make his own, as far as he could, at least some of the words which mark
the language of the Cymry. He did all this as a practising artist, working
with both verbal and visual images. These three strands come together in
a remarkable way in a letter written to Aneirin Talfan Davies, who had
asked his opinion on the reasons for 'the passion for the intricate and
complex' to be found in Celtic works of art, whether in *The Book of
Kells* or James Joyce's *Finnegans Wake*.

Jones begins with his usual disclaimer. 'Well, Aneirin, I fear I have
just *no* idea.' Then he goes on for ten pages, gradually feeling his way
towards some kind of statement on the subject There is, he says, a
desire in all works of art, but particularly in the Celtic world, to include
everything, the whole '*mewn lle bychan* . . . I mean the entirety or totality in a little place or space'. He quotes a part of the Gradual for the
Mass of the Eve of the Assumption *quem totus non capit orbis, in tua se
clausit viscera factus homo*: 'he whom the whole world cannot contain,
made man lies enclosed in your womb', thus making a clear analogy
between the work of art which sums up much in little, and the incarnation itself in which heaven and earth are contained in a little space. He
goes on:

> We want to say of this poem or that picture that that which the whole world
> cannot comprehend or hold has been enclosed within the strict confines of
> this or that *cerdd* (song or poem), *celfyddydwaith* (artefact), *cerfddelw*
> (sculpture), *llun* (picture), or *delw* (image) or any of the 'carpentries of
> song' that chaps have done and do no matter what the *trai a llanw* (the ebb
> and flow) of the centuries.[4]

'I've thought', he says, 'that the artist's best text or motto is found in
that psalm (Laetatus sum, ps. CXXII Verse 3 in the Book of Common
Prayer, ps. CXXI in the Vulgate) about Jerusalem being builded as a city
whose parts are united in one.' Why in the Celtic world this should
involve such extraordinary intricacy and complexity, which would seem
to some to be exorbitant, even an indulgence, he does not know. He
simply registers that it is so 'in that the inter-joining (which is what, I

suppose, *chydgyssylltu* [*sic*] in the Welsh version of the psalms means) is of unparalleled ingenuity and complexity in making a Celtic art work like a *dinas* (city) whose parts are united in one'.[5]

Well, it was true of his own works, this combination of unity and diversity, whether one thinks of a poem like *The Anathemata* or of a picture like *Trystan ac Essyllt*. The complexity sometimes seems to be exorbitant, yet always there is the desire that all should be safely gathered in; and in this man who did not know Welsh, and who tells us that he did not know Latin either, the Latin, the Celtic and the Anglo-Saxon elements which go to make up the heritage of this island are consciously held together and related to each other in a way which if it were more common would make our whole situation, political and social no less than cultural and spiritual, substantially less despairing, substantially more hopeful than at present it is.

Notes

[1] Valerie Wynne-Williams (née Price) was herself a friend of, and correspondent with, David Jones.

[2] *Sobornost*, a Russian word meaning Catholicity or collegiality, is the title of the journal of the Fellowship of St Alban and St Sergius, an ecumenical association of Christians of East and West, founded in 1928.

[3] Before I was born my parents lived in Northwick Park Road where Jones's private hotel was. My two elder brothers were born there. This is the kind of coincidence which greatly intrigued David Jones.

[4] It is not clear in Aneirin Talfan Davies's edition, prepared when the editor was critically ill, whether the bracketed English words of explanation were in the original or not; I suspect they were not.

[5] Aneirin Talfan Davies, *David Jones: Letters to a Friend* (Swansea: Christopher Davies, 1980), pp.81–2.

Images of National Renewal in 'The Sleeping Lord'

GERAINT EVANS

'The Sleeping Lord' is a poem which offers images of national renewal to a culture which David Jones constructs as having been embattled immemorially. For Jones, Welsh culture has been fighting the odds since it emerged as a distinct linguistic entity nearly two thousand years ago, and his work foregrounds the fact that images of this struggle go back at least as far as the time commemorated in its earliest surviving poetic texts. Of the poems now known to us as *hengerdd*, Jones had a favourite, to which he kept referring in all aspects of his work: a group of heroic elegies, known as the *Gododdin*,[1] which tell of a defeat so overwhelming that virtually none survived but the poet who recorded the events. The *Gododdin* was also interesting to Jones because it contained an early reference to Arthur, but its main significance is that in much of Jones's work, of which I take 'The Sleeping Lord' to be typical, assertions of cultural value and survival, together with images of national renewal, are often presented in terms of heroic failure, of which Arthur is here the exemplar. Viewed within the context of the nationalist movement in Wales since the 1920s, this type of writing represents a potentially self-defeating, albeit poignantly elegiac, paradigm of history.

Jones's poem 'The Sleeping Lord' was completed between November 1966 and March 1967 and published in 1974 as the title poem in a book of what he called 'poetic fragments', despite their being in many ways linked thematically and stylistically to each other and to much of his previous work.[2] The argument of the poem is straightforward: the narrative voice considers the location and manner of the entombment of Arthur, the sleeping lord of the title, and this meditation frames a central section which recreates some of the characters and rituals which, in Jones's version, surrounded Arthur during his earthly life.

Jones constructs a version of early, and by implication, of modern Welsh life as a seamless and natural unity containing a number of very specific elements. Each piece which is added to the picture – each historical or literary or linguistic element – helps to construct a view of history, not only in what is added, but also in what is not added. Having an Arthur who takes Mass and speaks Welsh reclaims for Wales a universalized hero while denying two of the most popular of modern Welsh stereotypes: the rural Nonconformist and the English-speaking southerner. It is also important to remember that Jones's view of Wales is one which evolved over many years and which he endlessly rehearsed and refined, a practice which helps to explain the apparently seamless final version. So in constructing his particular version of Welsh history, in the 'The Sleeping Lord', as in *The Anathemata*, *The Dying Gaul*, the later inscriptions and many of the letters, a number of elements recur. For Jones, Welsh culture is defined by a society which is Welsh-speaking, aristocratic, pre-Tudor, Catholic, residually Romanized and, overwhelmingly, defeated.

In refining this view of the Welsh tradition, in the thirty years or so between the publication of his first book *In Parenthesis*, and the writing of 'The Sleeping Lord', Jones was greatly influenced by Saunders Lewis, with whom he corresponded occasionally from 1937 and regularly from the mid-1950s. Jones was forever asking Lewis for translations of words or phrases into or out of Welsh, and for opinions about this poet and that event, and about the relative stature of historical figures such as Glyndŵr and Llywelyn ap Gruffudd. Jones and Lewis became close friends and came to share a view of post-medieval Wales as rather a poor creature. Saunders Lewis regarded the fifteenth century generally as a golden age in Europe and 1350–1550 as the golden age of Welsh poetry, positions which Jones came to share, positions which are not unconnected with a desire to recover the Catholic element of the Welsh tradition which had been so marginalized by the ascendant Nonconformist orthodoxy.

The poem opens, as it concludes, with a series of rhetorical questions where phrases and clauses, all beginning with grammatical items, are strung together in an enumeration of the Arthurian mysteries:

> And is his bed wide
> is his bed deep on the folded strata
> is his bed long
> where is his bed and
> where has he lain him
> from north of Llanfair-ym-Muallt
> (a name of double-gladius-piercings)
> south of the carboniferous vaulting of Gwyr. (*SL*, 70)

This is the basic process of narrative development in the opening and closing sections – a series of rhetorical questions about Arthur's resting place which lead, via a description of the court, to a completely new meaning for modern Wales of the significance of the myth of the sleeping lord, who is ready to return in his country's darkest hour. The opening also locates the text in a number of important ways. First of all the 'folded strata' and 'carboniferous vaulting' introduce the notion of prehistory, so that from its opening sentence the poem is addressing a condition which is larger than a historically placed Arthur, a device which is familiar from the opening section of *The Anathemata* (1952). The opening lines also contain a number of closely controlled devices which foreground certain ideas and begin to establish points of closure. Most significantly, there is the repetition of the phrase 'is his bed' in each of the first four lines which leads, through the release from repetition, to the crucial fifth line: 'and/where has he lain him', an active construction which affirms Arthur's being alive: a corpse is laid by others in a tomb; a merely sleeping warrior lays himself down to rest and can consequently rise again.

The heroic construction of Arthur as literally larger than life is established in questions about the bed being wide and deep and long, but these are also part of the construction and closure which prepares the reader for the topographical metaphor of the poem's final lines. Jones's work also uses devices well known from other modernist epics. For example, opening a poem about history with the word 'and' recalls the opening of Ezra Pound's 'Canto 1': 'And then went down to the ship / Set keel to breakers, forth on the godly sea . . .'[3] This device denies that it is in fact a beginning by referring to events which precede the opening of the text. Where Jones is interesting, though, and in English perhaps unique amongst modernists, is in the large number of formal and linguistic allusions not to classical culture but to the Welsh tradition. He chooses to bound the area of Arthur's resting at Llanfair ym Muallt as he calls him in a footnote which echoes the title, the Lord Llywelyn, who also sleeps nearby at Abaty-Cwm-hir (*SL*, 71). Furthermore, Jones is laying great stress on the precise location of the resting place being unknown: '. . . is his bed wide / is [it] deep / is [it] long / where is [it]?' recalling not only a specifically Welsh element of the Arthur story from *Englynion y Beddau*, 'anoeth byd bedd Arthur',[4] but also that other warrior hero whose grave is unknown and around whom legends form: Glyndŵr. And the point of these skilfully intertwined references is that the text is arguing that history constructs for us a model of Welsh heroism in which all these elements are recurring and significant, and the most significant is that while in each age a warrior hero emerges to rally the people, he is always, ultimately, defeated. And when we consider the cultural significance of texts like 'The Sleeping Lord' in (to paraphrase Kenneth O. Morgan) the political rebirth of a nation, it is politically significant that such a key figure as Saunders Lewis, with his interest in Distributism, his apparent fondness for monarchy and his elevation of fifteenth-century social organization, should have been an admirer of, and a contributor to, a text which is central to this particular version of history. To return to 'The Sleeping Lord', I am saying that the text argues that history constructs for us a model of heroism – but history *per se*, that is, lived experience, does not argue anything. Texts alone, through selection, juxtaposition and closure argue a position or urge a cause. Given an infinite amount of information, the simple act of selection involved in recording one thing rather than another challenges our whole notion of objectivity.

So texts like 'The Sleeping Lord' have as one of their central characteristics of Wales and Welshness these paradigms of heroic defeat. In other works, such as *In Parenthesis* (1937), Jones concentrates on the battle of Catraeth, described in the *Gododdin* poems, but while the emphasis varies, the function is the same. Furthermore, many of the references of defeat are very deeply embedded in the text and are not just tacked on as simple quotation. Surely the repeated questions, 'does his . . . does he . . . do you', in a poem about a buried hero, are meant to recall for the Welsh reader the lament of Llywelyn ap Gruffudd by Gruffudd ab yr Ynad Coch, with its repeated question 'poni welwch . . . poni welwch . . .' (do you not see . . . do you not see . . .).[5]

Another characteristic feature of all Jones's texts – letters, poems, essays, inscriptions – is the careful interweaving of non-English words and phrases, usually Welsh and Latin, into the English text. It is clear from manuscripts preserved in the National Library of Wales, Aberystwyth, that Jones produced texts in more or less the same manner whatever they were, and that texts which apparently inhabit different formal and social contexts tend to rehearse and construct similar subject positions. In letters, he tries out ideas which later appear in poems or essays, and even more interestingly, he writes numerous drafts of letters, many of which survive, until the desired effect is achieved. There are, for example, numerous drafts of a letter, which may never even have been sent, to a person Jones had never met, who wrote to him once praising *The Anathemata*. But the significance of this for the Welsh element in his work is that drafts of letters and poems clearly show that he meticulously checked phrasing and spelling and mutation in order to present the multilingual text as natural and automatic. (This practice is equally true for the other non-modern English words and phrases, for example, in Latin or Middle English.) Phrases like 'hope that's right' and 'if I remember it properly' which pepper his correspondence, nearly always occur with items he has been able to check and therefore knows to be correct. Disclaimers rarely accompany mistakes, and the occasional unglossed infelicities in the manuscripts are sufficient to show the work which went into producing the final published texts. So his whole effort in a work like 'The Sleeping Lord' is to introduce into the devices and idiolect of twentieth-century English modernist writing, words and phrases which are redolent of Brythonic Romanity, and to make the result seamless:

> should this *candela*-bearer
>   presume so far as to argue that
> his *cannwyll* does indeed constitute
> One of the Three Primary Signa
>   of the Son of Mary
> . . . *unig-anedig Fab Duw*
>   . . . *ante omnia saecura*
> *lumen de lumine* . . .
>   by whom all things . . .
> who should blame him? (*SL*, 77)

And later: 'or whether the same anamnesis was made in the *capel frenhinol*, / . . . as here and now, in the Bear's chapel' (*SL*, 81), so that the constant juxtaposition of Welsh and Latin elements in an imperial or Catholic context argues not only for a version of history in which Wales is predominantly not a Protestant country but also maintains that the enduring, significant, cultural inheritance which the language preserves is firstly Brythonic, secondly continental, and therefore in no primary way English.

Reverting for a moment to Saunders Lewis and the shared interest in pre-Tudor, Catholic Wales, this is a device for making a version of Wales which effectively ends at 1536 but begins again with a series of nationalist revivals and which, by the mid-twentieth century, is emerging, largely unaffected by the English interlude:

And next, his rapid memento is of those lords & rulers and men of name in the land in times past: *penmilwyr, aergwn, aergyfeddau, cymdeithion yn y ffosydd, cadfridogion, tribuni militum, pennaethau, comitates, rhiau, cadflaenoriaid, sub-reguli*, pendragons, *protectores, rhaglawiaid, strategoi, duces*, saviours & leaders of varying eminence together with *gwyr o galon* of all sorts. (*SL*, 81)

Throughout 'The Sleeping Lord' there are a large number of non-English words and phrases which delineate the areas of experience which, in the standard modernist way, a reader is constructed as possessing. In Jones's work, these insertions are nearly all noun phrases, apart from liturgical or biblical quotations where the text can be quoted directly. They are phrases like: 'the tough, gnarled *derwen*' (oak); 'the fragile *blodyn y gwynt*' (wood anemone); 'below in the *glynnoedd*' (valleys or glens); 'where the *nentydd* run' (streams) (*SL*, 74). And in most cases, certainly in the four quoted above, the text is printed with the Welsh phrase in italics, further drawing attention to the mixture of languages and experience which he is hoping to signify. Moreover, the Welsh element consists almost entirely of lexical items. Even in an unusually long example like '. . . green-budding boughs moan and complain afresh to each other *yn y gaeaf oer* (in the cold winter) . . .' (*SL*, 76) the grammatical items are merely completing a phrase of which the significant element is the two lexical items, *gaeaf* (winter) and *oer* (cold). I would suggest that this practice, as it is repeated every few lines, amounts to a rhetorical device in which the narrative voice is implying: 'which we of this island call *gaeaf*', 'which we of this island call *oer*'. The narrative voice is operating, however competent or sophisticated it may be, outside an exclusively English tradition. Elsewhere in the poem, the narrative voice says: '. . . and when he comes to the words which in the other tongue of men / of the Island signify *trwy Iesu Grist ein Hargwlydd* . . .',[6] cleverly foregrounding both Latin and Welsh at the expense of English: the spoken words are Latin but what they signify is Welsh, apparently 'the other tongue . . . of the island', but implicitly 'our tongue'.

Jones, then, uses not only historical characters and events, but also linguistic and stylistic elements, to create a version of Welsh history which defines Welsh culture very specifically, and which seems to offer the possibility of hope and renewal. In using characters such as Arthur, and, elsewhere, Owain Glyndŵr and Llywelyn ap Gruffudd, he is arguing that heroic exemplars exist, and that continued struggle could be facilitated by the habitual remembrance of them. The problem as I see it is that for all the foregrounding of Welsh tradition and the delineation of its continental cognates, and however successfully the recently dominant English culture is marginalized, texts like 'The Sleeping Lord' risk creating a nostalgic attachment to paradigms of history which are based on cycles of struggle and failure: they are texts which are so deeply conservative that they cannot accommodate any lasting change to the status quo.

As the poem reaches its conclusion, the magical picture of Arthurian life finally gives way to the rhetorical refrain which opened the poem, with the imagined, lost world of Arthur revealed but not yet regained:

> But yet he sleeps:
> when he shifts a little in his fitful
> slumber does a covering stone dislodge
> and roll to Reynoldstone?
> When he fretfully turns
> crying out in a great voice
> his fierce sleep-anger
> does the habergeon'd sentinel
> alert himself? (*SL*, 94)

The initial pattern of layered questions reasserts itself:

> Does he cock his weather-ear . . .
> Does he nudge his drowsing mate? . . .
> Yet he sleeps on
> very deep is his slumber:
> how long has he been the sleeping lord? (*SL*, 95–6)

And the poem leads us to the final achievement of Jones's argument, that there is a version of Wales and of Welshness which history reveals to us, and which may contain the seeds of national renewal in a metaphorical reading of the old legend:

> Are the slumbering valleys . . .
> him in slumber . . .
> . . . or is the wasted land
> that very lord who sleeps? (*SL*, 96)

In 'The Sleeping Lord' there is a clear, united expression of ideas, which occur repeatedly in other David Jones texts, and which are representative of a more general semiotic of national renewal throughout the twentieth century in Wales. The argument is largely created in 'The Sleeping Lord' by one of Jones's principal poetic devices – the juxtaposition of elements and events from Welsh and non-Welsh tradition, and the weaving of Welsh words and phrases into what is essentially an English modernist text. In doing this Jones creates poems which argue that history reveals to us a true version of Wales and of Welshness if only the past is read in the right way. But the past, as it is represented in 'The Sleeping Lord', might be offering something less than a vision of renewal. The figure of Arthur is only one of a number of elements which are used to create a version of Welsh history whose most

significant characteristic is not successful rebuilding or achieved independence but poignant, heroic defeat.

Notes

[1] Ifor Williams, *Canu Aneirin* (Cardiff: University of Wales Press, 1938).

[2] David Jones, *The Sleeping Lord* (London: Faber, 1974). Subsequent page
number references to the 'The Sleeping Lord' in my text refer to this edition.

[3] Ezra Pound, *Cantos 1–117* (London: Faber, 1975).

[4] Literally 'unknown is Arthur's grave'.

[5] Jones's principal sources of the poem were Thomas Parry's Welsh text in *The
Oxford Book of Welsh Verse* (Oxford: Oxford University Press, 1962) and Gwyn
Williams's translation in *The Burning Tree* (London: Faber, 1956).

[6] 'Through Jesus Christ our Lord' (*SL*, 79).

Feminist Principles in David Jones's Art

ANNE PRICE-OWEN

If, as Kate Campbell claims, 'feminism ... is about nothing if not ending women's inequality, oppression and subordination',[1] then a case may be made for David Jones as a feminist writer and artist. Nevertheless, it is not enough to state that because he dissolved the barriers between the sexes, Jones may be viewed as a feminist. In both his literature and visual work, there is a distinct blending of male and female personages which inevitably incurs role reversal. Although a healthy feminist trait, this does not in itself constitute feminism. However, by investigating some feminist concepts in relation to Jones's work, I wish to demonstrate Jones's feminist thinking. For this purpose I shall focus on what I consider is Jones's greatest feminist painting: *Aphrodite in Aulis* (1941) (frontispiece), and draw parallels between this and his literary work.

In his placing of Aphrodite, the semi-nude goddess of love, who is larger than life and perched precariously on a pedestal, Jones isolates her from the remaining content of this picture. Her central, elevated position, together with her outsize scale in relation to the surrounding figures, is comparable to the conventional position of early Renaissance Madonnas. There the cursory resemblance ends. The figure's dishevelled appearance, the garter on her left leg, the mesh glove, the rings together with flimsy, transparent clothing suggest she is a courtesan. Jones confirms that his original intention was to make a picture of Phryne, one of the two courtesans specified in *The Anathemata* (180).[2] Subsequently, Jones changed his mind about the subject's identity and created a sacrificial female figure associated with Aulis, the city where Agamemnon was ordered to sacrifice his daughter for the sake of the Greek fleet which was weather-bound in the harbour. Hence Iphigeneia is depicted, but because Jones wished 'to include *all* female cult-figures as ... the figure is all goddesses rolled into one',[3] he substituted Aphrodite, Greek goddess of love, for Iphigeneia.

This is an example of Jones's propensity for presenting women in their traditional roles. These are roles to which many feminists are averse, namely that of Virgin and/or Whore, or the chaste and the unchaste woman. Immediately this introduces the question of sexuality, which in our culture has customarily been the cause of difference and inequality between the sexes. Deborah Thom maintains that

> feminism has given history an enormously improved understanding of one of the fundamental divides in society, the one between the sexes, and it has given an improved understanding of why it is that a divide is also a structure of dominance; and that uncomfortable truth means the impropriety remains, the grit which continues to produce the pearls.[4]

Using the metaphor of pearls, Jones goes one step further than Thom by identifying Helen of Troy as 'the pearl-to-be-sought within the traversed and echeloned defences of the city' (*A*, 54 n.1). This is reflected in the additional symbolism in the painting, where the crescent moon is like an extension of Aphrodite's head, emphasizing her association with Helen, the moon, tree and light goddesses (*A*, 191 n.3), and the pre-Christian archetype for all females of that name. In *The Anathemata*, the Virgin Mary's affinity with these foretypes is posited:

> She's as she of Aulis, master:
> not a puff of wind without her!
> her fiat is our fortune, sir: like Helen's face
> t'was that as launched the ship. (128)

Their fiat, decree, or as Thom would argue 'grit' is what Jones relies on in order to endow his women with metamorphosis which elevates them from the mundane to the admirable. For the grit to produce the pearl a container is implied. In Helen's case, Troy's city walls contain her. This concept of woman as restricted, and in some wise restrained, concurs with Lynda Nead's thesis that the female body is contained and therefore perceived within outlines, margins and frames.[5] In his early visual work, especially his engravings, Jones appears to advance this traditional (male) view of women, where strong outlines constrain the figure. Although this may be a by-product of the engraver's medium, Jones adopts the same treatment in his drawings (fig. 9).

By 1930 Jones's pictorial style had undergone a radical change, whereby the bold delineation was replaced by tenuous, sensitive lines and strokes which suggest the female figure is at one with her environment (fig. 12). This is largely due to the fluid, transient quality of Jones's paintings. Consequently, he subverts the suggestion of confinement in his figures, creating instead a powerful sense of unity between

Fig. 9: David Jones, *Elizabeth, Petra and Joanna Gill* (1924)

forms, as evidenced also in his interiors, still lifes and landscapes of this period.

Despite releasing his depictions of women from their stereotypical boundaries, Jones continued to view women as ideal persons, elevated, on a pedestal, almost untouchable, remote and even to be revered individuals. In his poetry women are metaphors for vessels and containers. They themselves are contained or protected, but are simultaneously presented as tutelars: they are both protected and guardians. These paradoxical functions are found in Jones's concept of womankind, manifested in the Virgin Mary, who is the assimilation of her foretypes, for example Demeter the mother goddess, and Helen the ancient tree goddess. Mythic, or actual, heroines and saints, such as Persephone, Iphigeneia, Helen of Troy, Sts Bridget and Helen, are also idealized embodiments of womankind.

Alternatively (and often simultaneously), Jones also portrays women as courtesans, like Phryne, and also as individuals who personify our heritage, for example Blodeuedd, Gwenever and Iseult. All are women of exceptional beauty, and with somewhat loose sexual morals, comparable to Venus, and also to *The Anathemata*'s central figure, the Lady of the Pool. In these characters he also identified redeeming features, thus transforming them from the profane to the sacred, making them worthy, even ideal. This is hardly surprising for, as J. Williams remarks,

> Women have been seen as incarnations of both the highest good and the basest evil, of chastity and of lust, of virtue and deceit, and the sacred and the profane. Men, and women, who are co-opted by the prevalent male view, have rarely been able to perceive women simply as human beings with the same range of idiosyncrasies as themselves. Rather, they have had to make myths to explain their awesome differences and their strange powers.[6]

Often, Jones uses mythopoeic associations in referring to women in both his poetry and painting for the reasons Williams gives. In addition, Jones creates combinations which displace, even dislocate, the female characters of his art so that sometimes they become figments of his imagination, as in *Escaping Figure with Trinkets* (*c.* 1939) (fig. 10), a voluptuous, sexy woman protecting the 'blessed things that have taken on what is cursed and the profane things that somehow are redeemed' (*A*, 28–9). Many of the women Jones portrays actually existed, like his friend and patron Prudence Pelham (1930) (fig. 11), whom Jones depicts comfortably in her surroundings, and with the dignity of her archetype *Prudentia*. But in his portrait of Petra Gill, his one time fiancée, entitled *Petra im Rosenhag* (1931) (fig. 12) real and imagined are conjoined to evoke a picture of the Madonna in a rose garden. This is Jones imposing his vision of the ideal on a particular woman.

The identity of Jones's sitters hardly matters: what Jones renders is a human image of a concept. Ultimately, he was concerned with expressing the essence of man*kind* which he demonstrates by interchanging the roles of men and women. Here it is worth distinguishing between what Jones calls 'the feminine principle' and my discussion of feminist principles. Jeremy Hooker sums up his interpretation of Jones's use of the feminine principle thus:

> The concept of a female principle is . . . open to various interpretations . . . For Jones it means tenderness . . . and all creaturely and kindly qualities; and it means the chthonic powers, the primary creative force in nature: both what man is in part, and what he is utterly dependent on . . . It is nature as woman, and woman as nature; but it means the equality of total interdependence too, and wit and intellect and force of personality.[7]

This definition, where man- and womankind are interdependent, share character traits and where both are instruments of creativity, has a great deal in common with feminist aspirations. Such ideals are possible, for as Toril Moi comments:

Fig. 10: David Jones, *Escaping Figure with Trinkets* (late 1930s)

Fig. 11: David Jones, *Prudence Pelham* (1930)

The real strength of the women's liberation movement is not that of having laid claim to the specificity of their sexuality and the rights pertaining to it, but that they have actually departed from the discourse conducted within the apparatuses of sexuality ... a veritable movement of desexualisation, a displacement effected in relation to the sexual centring of the problem, formulating the demand for forms of culture, discourse, language, and so on, which are no longer part of that rigid assignation and pinning-down to their sex which they had initially in some sense been politically obliged to accept in order to make themselves heard.[8]

By examining Jones's methods of construction, and the content of his works, his affinity with feminist goals may be clarified. Like feminists' works, Jones's art seeks to redress cultural imbalances: he does not dwell on gender distinctions but rather blurs the edges of sexuality. This often results in one gender appropriating the characteristics of its complementary. By implication, Jones's art is a synthesis of his attempt to transform society, facilitate social change and eliminate inequality between men and women.

This message is particularly evident in Jones's poetry where ambiguities and puns are commonplace, and extend the meaning of the whole work. The verse is informed by themes which also predominate in the visual work. Jones continually cites women's strengths and triumphs, which are frequently superior to those of men. His concept of women is not entirely radical, however, for he simultaneously presents women in traditional guises, as creatures of refuge and comfort, as agents for what he terms 'the kind and the creaturely'. The feminine principle exists in men as well as women, just as the masculine principle – characterized by the aggressive instinct – is manifest, and I use the epithet deliberately, in women. Nevertheless, Jones seldom projects the masculine instincts in his women, whom he invariably views as mothers (notably Mary, Eve, Demeter, Tellus Mater, Mother Earth), as daughters (Helen of Troy, Persephone, Iphigeneia), as sisters (Elizabeth, Margaret, Helen of the Hosts), as wives (Mary, bride of Christ, Helen, wife of Constantine, Gwenever, wife of Arthur, and also Iseult, wife of Mark), and as lovers (the Queen of the Woods, the Lady of the Pool – Elen Monica – Eve, Phryne and also Mary, 'lover' of Christ).

Such a catalogue of names strengthens Jones's complex notion of woman which is essentially one of mother and carer, for as he declares in 'The Sleeping Lord':

> She that loves place, time, demarcation, hearth, kin, enclosure,
> site, differentiated cult, though she is but one mother of us all ...

Fig. 12: David Jones, *Petra im Rosenhag* (1931)

Tellus of the myriad names answers to but one name . . .

                    Man-travail and woman-war here we
see enacted are.

Though she inclines with attention from far fair-height outside
all boundaries, beyond the known and kindly nomenclatures,
where all names are one name, where all stones of demarcation
dance and interchange. (59–60)

Clearly, Jones is not content with promulgating disunity, but seeks for a
way to unify the diverse strands by ultimately conflating these individuals into Mary, the quintessence of the female principle, and, I would
argue, the embodiment of the feminist cause, because she bore Christ
without the aid of a man!

In the painting *Aphrodite in Aulis*, the structure is circular and may be
compared to that of *The Anathemata*, which begins and ends with the
Mass. This is not surprising, for, as Paul Hills notes, many of Jones's
later compositions are based around a central axis, and the circle is
implied.[9] Moreover, the circularity of the composition is realized in its
representational features: the goddess occupies the centre of a semicircular temple. Circular and semicircular shapes are repeated and
reflected throughout the work, whether in the coils on the capitals, the
accoutrements of battle, like the shield and the horn, the crescent moon,
and even in the woman's right breast as well as the shape of her face.

The circle has for long been an archetypal symbol of the female.
Figuratively speaking it may be seen to represent the cave of refuge, that
is the cleft, or fissure, in the rock, the *agelastos petra* associated with
Demeter (*A*, 92). The cleft also appears in the painting. Situated on the
upper left in the hillside, it lies at right angles to the tip of the spear
carried by the soldier left of Aphrodite. The proximity of the spear, or
what Jessie Weston refers to as the phallus,[10] to the cleft, which Jones
avers is a symbol of the female genitalia (*A*, 56 n. 1), is intentional. It is
through the union of these opposites that new life issues, that renascence
takes place.

Moreover, the cave or cleft is 'Liknites' cave of bread' (*A*, 232),
cognate also with Bethlehem 'House of Flesh' (*A*, 232 n. 2). Therefore
the physical material of the cave, depending on its alternative associations with womb or tomb, is either flesh or stone. The correspondence
between bread and Christ are obvious, but the cave also symbolizes
Mary's womb which 'cavern'd Christ' (*A*, 225). Thus Jones intimates
that the refuge is not only life-giving, but also that it is both male and
female. He advances this concept when describing the cave, or tomb, in

which Christ was buried. Accordingly, the cave stands for birth, thus suggesting the feminine, but also its opposite, death. Death is a means to life, and Jones unifies these contraries in the final part of *In Parenthesis*, where the Queen of the Woods is the agent for both death and regeneration. The injured John Ball crawls deeper into the refuge of the wood (and we may take it that wood has all the connotations Jones outlines in his Preface to *The Anathemata* (23)), but the wood is a tomb and final resting place for most of Ball's companions. In addition, the tomb doubles as a womb, as the last verse testifies:

> Oeth and Annoeth's hosts they were
> who in that night grew
> younger men
> younger striplings. (*IP*, 187)

In his painting of Aphrodite, the goddess resembles the Queen of the Woods, in that her garments comprise shimmering foliage and blossoms; even a rose has fallen onto her plinth, she is 'so wholly super-pellised of ... wild woods' (*A*, 203). Jones's tendency for conflating percepts equates with his predilection for maximizing on concepts. Aphrodite is a complex assimilation of

> all female cult-figures ... She is 'Elen the bracelet-giver' of *I[n] P[aren-thesis]* also, & also the many-wounded Mair, Rhiannon of the *Mabinogion* ... [as well as Gwenever of the Arthurian legend] ... the Lady of the Pool refers to Our Lady as comprehending in herself all the potent pre-Xian cult-figures and their sufferings.[11]

However, because she is in Aulis, she is really Iphigeneia, Agamemnon's faithful daughter. As a portrait of sacrifice, the painting recalls Christ's sacrifice, and the stigmata would seem to verify this. Moreover, the column on which the goddess stands bears the motif of the Agnus Dei with the pierced side from which blood and water flow into the cup below. Aphrodite, therefore, must be a figure for Mary of whom Simeon predicted: 'Yea, and a sword shall pierce thine own soul also.'[12] Nevertheless, Jones's original intention was to paint a picture of the courtesan, Phryne, who was redeemed by her beauty at her trial. He modelled his female on the memory of a plaster cast of the Venus de Milo, from his art school days. According to the texture he simulates in the painting, he creates a marble figure, thus transforming the woman into Gwenever, who is likened to a marble pillar in *The Anathemata* (202ff.). The analogy between Venus and Phryne, and subsequently Gwenever, is sustained in the text for, as in the painting: 'We are not concerned with portrait but it can be inferred that of / her eyes, one was blemished' (*A*, 202). This is a distinguishing feature of Aphrodite (*A*, 194 n. 2). The blemish is also a metaphor for transgression; thus Phryne is implicated, as is Gwenever for her infidelity to Arthur. Jones puns on the word gilt when describing her hair, which also applies to his image of Aphrodite:

> If her gilt, unbound
> (for she was consort of a *regulus*) and falling to below her
> sacral bone, was pale as standing . . . barley-corn, here, held back
> in the lunula of Doleucothi gold, it was paler than the under-
> stalks of barley, held in the sickle's lunula. So that the pale
> gilt, where it was by nature palest, together with the pale river-
> gold where it most received the pallid candle-sheen, rimmed
> the crescent whiteness where it was whitest.
> Or, was there already silver to the gilt?
>
> . . .
>
> . . . for she was the spouse of the Director of Toil, and,
> because of the toil within,
> her temples gleamed
> among the carried lights hard-contoured as Luna's rim . . . (*A*, 196–7)

With a typical male gaze, Jones sees her as unchaste. But this is a marble character, whom Jones subsequently describes as a

> whole leaning column (which was the live base for [the
> magnificent clothes] . . . that sheathed . . . the breathing marble,
> . . . leaned, and toward the Stone. (*A*, 202–3)

In the poetic context, the column is Gwenever, an alias for Mary, while the Stone is Christ. In a devious reversal of roles, Jones also implies that Mary personifies the stone in exclaiming: 'No wonder the proud column leaned . . . over the Stone . . . By whom also this column was' (*A*, 204–5).

I believe that Jones intentionally upsets the traditional gender balance. The column is an archetypal symbol of masculinity, but Jones is refer- ring to Gwenever. The stone, as I have illustrated, may be interpreted as the tomb, a female symbol, and Jones manipulates the paradoxes of power relations between the sexes. In other words, he rejects what Virginia Woolf describes as 'the sentence made by men' which is loose, heavy and pompous.[13] 'Sentence' may be read as a metaphor for the ways men perceived women as well as the style in which they wrote. Woolf insisted that the female writer nurture her own personal creativity to reflect herself, 'altering and adapting the current sentence until she writes one that takes the natural shape of her thought without crushing or distorting it'.[14] In the ensuing quotation I have replaced Woolf's female pronoun by the masculine, because what she says of Dorothy Richardson is applicable to Jones:

> [He] has invented . . . developed and applied to [his] own use, a sentence which we might call the psychological sentence of the feminine gender. It is of a more elastic fibre than the old, capable of stretching to the extreme, of suspending the frailest particles, of enveloping the vaguest of shapes.[15]

In the previous passage on Gwenever, Jones's elasticity, that is, his ability to return to the metaphor of the moon without upsetting the overall tension of the verse, is demonstrated. Further, he suspends the colour motifs while retaining the underlying theme of gilt and guilt. The subsequent stanzas which I quote may be examined in a similar light.

Virginia Woolf's advice to women writers would seem to question Janet Wolff's hypothesis that 'a fundamental opposition exists between those women who wish to project a positive and celebratory image of women, such as the visual artists, Judy Chicago and Nancy Spero', and

> women who employ the various media to deconstruct dominant meanings, problematising issues of gender and opening up spaces for women to articulate their experiences . . . The celebratory work often revives traditional female crafts, or uses the female body as a vehicle and subject matter, and is too often naively essentialist. Also, it misses the point that in a patriarchal culture it is not possible simply to declare a kind of unilateral independence. The guerrilla tactics of engaging with that regime and undermining it with 'destabilising' strategies (collage, juxtaposition, reappropriation of the image, etc.) provide the most effective possibility for feminist art practices today.[16]

Jones, perhaps because he is a man, is involved with both these processes. On the one hand, he celebrates women and often appears to be 'naively essentialist' in representing virgin-types. On the other, he employs 'destabilizing' devices in order to subvert the traditional ideal by foregrounding women's indiscretions. This is evident in his poetry, which may be favourably compared with the painterly techniques specified by Wolff. In fact, Margaret Iversen develops Wolff's statement, convinced that 'by adopting collage or montage or scripto-visual techniques, one could present the conditions and causes of women's oppression instead of simply reproducing its appearances'.[17]

In both art forms, I would argue, Jones simulates the effects of collage, montage and scripto-visual techniques, despite the fact that with the possible exception of some of his painted inscriptions, he seldom uses them in the literal sense. In his poetry he juxtaposes similes and also puns on words to maximize their ambiguities, while yet retaining accurate and often interchangeable meanings, so that the connotative value is compounded. In changing his style of expression to suit the characters' personae and accents, and by combining poetry and prose to a masterly degree, Jones communicates the lyricism, or urgency, or pathos, or celebration, of his varied literary style.

Because the content of his visual works often displays arresting juxta-positions, and is frequently permeated by a shape-shifting, transient quality, montage is suggested. So much of his pictorial work depends on his devotion to language, its comprehension and ambiguities, that Jones can scarcely put pencil to paper without evoking religious, literary or historical themes and characters. His painted inscriptions (figs. 7 and 8) express Iversen's composite definition in terms of painterly skills, as well as illustrating the way Jones's mind worked.

This is why Jones's image of the marble woman in *Aphrodite in Aulis* may be Mary, Venus, Gwenever, Phryne and a host of other women from the past, whether fact or fiction. And she is a figure for Christ, who also stands for Love. Her position on the altar which continues the upward thrust of the pillar, the stigmata, the severed manacle symboliz-ing the broken chain of evil, and the priest censing the altar, confirm the affiliation. Moreover, the soldiers on either side are reminiscent of the soldiers at the foot of the Cross.

Both soldiers carry instruments of aggression: the spear and the rifle, respectively. The British soldier's spear leans towards the statue in the same way that Gwenever inclined towards the column, while the German soldier appears to cradle his rifle away from the main figure. In *In Parenthesis* Jones suggests that the rifle is feminine by the intimate vocabulary he uses to persuade the soldier to care for it:

> it's the soldier's best friend if you care for the working parts
> and . . . really cultivate the habit of treating this weapon with the
> very greatest care and there should be a healthy rivalry among
> you – it should be a matter of very proper pride and   . (183)

The break here hardly prepares us for the shock which follows when Jones insists on the marriage between the soldier and his rifle as commanded by Sergeant Quilter:

> Marry it man! Marry it!
> Cherish her, she's your very own.
>   Coax it man coax it – it's delicately and ingeniously made
> – it's an instrument of precision . . .
>   Fondle it . . . talk to it – consider it as you would
> a friend –. (183–4)

The devotion the soldier experiences for his rifle is articulated through
John Ball's language which evokes that used by lovers:

> You've known her hot and cold.
> You would choose her from among many.
> You know her by her bias, and by her exact error at 300, and
> by the deep scar at the small, by the fair flaw in the grain. (184)

Ball, although wounded and weighed down by his rifle, registers his
loyalty for the weapon in his reluctance to cast it aside:

> It's difficult with the weight of the rifle.
> Leave it – under the oak.
> Leave it for a salvage-bloke
> let it lie bruised for a monument
> dispense the authenticated fragments to the faithful. (183)
>
>
> . . .
> but leave it under the oak.
>
> Slung so, it swings its full weight. With you going blindly on
> all paws, it slews its whole length, to hang at your bowed neck
> like the Mariner's white oblation. (184)
>
>   Let it lie for the dews to rust it, or ought you to decently
> cover the working parts.
>   Its dark barrel, where you leave it under the oak, reflects
> the solemn star that rises urgently . . .
>   It's a beautiful doll for us. (*IP*, 186)

The rifle the German carries in the painting, however, like the tin hat
of the British soldier, sprouts blossoms, so that it appears to be a visual
metaphor for 'the Blossom'd stem' (*A*, 188). Jones refers to the rod of
Jesse, and Christ's family tree, which is masculine, but its correspondence with the rifle transforms its gender. Even Aphrodite, as a column,
engages with this metaphor, because of the blossoms and her upright
posture. She is the sacrificial virgin and, in the Christian tradition, the

Virgin was a sign of the tree, or stem, as realized in the etymological associations: Latin *virga*, a stem being also cognate with Latin *virgo*, a virgin.

Jones arrives at this dense picture by building a series of layers of symbolism which cross-reference and interrelate with one another, somewhat in the technique of montage. Similarly, in his poetry he achieves an equally complex picture of associative characters by interspersing his text with quotations, paradoxes and ambiguities. For instance, the identity of the chosen child about whom:

> They say it's Tuesday child
> is chose
> this year's Mab o' the Green
> *mundi Domina*
> or was she Monday's
> total beauty
> *Stabat* by the Blossom'd Stem? (*A*, 188)

At first the child's gender is withheld, which implies that either Christ or Mary is the subject, both being full of grace. However, Jones's use of the feminine pronoun suggests that the child is Mary who is fair of face. He conjures up a picture of the May Queen ('Mab o' the Green') but implies that she is also Mary by the Latin quotation. But Mab, being Welsh for son, persuades me that the child is Christ. Moreover, Jones's concluding question is unanswered, indicating that the ambiguity surrounding the child's gender remains deliberately unresolved. Clearly, Jones is determined to establish and sustain the similitude between Mary and Christ.

This is reflected in the picture where the goddess (or is it Christ?) is being censed by a priest. The priest is a vicarious Christ, one of 'the dedicated men in skirts' (*A*, 179), thus compounding the interchangeable roles between men and women. This kind of reasoning also explains how Jones perceives unity in apparent oppositions, and how his individual images are independent of one another, yet are symbiotically interrelated, coherent and compatible.

Such a claim may appear to be about the paradox of unity which is perhaps best expressed by Marshall Berman, and which adequately sums up Jones's poetry and this painting:

A unity of disunity: it pours us all into a maelstrom of perpetual disintegration and renewal, of struggle and contradiction, of ambiguity and anguish. To be modern is to be part of a universe in which, as Marx said 'All that is solid melts into air'.[18]

Notes

[1] Kate Campbell (ed.), *Critical Feminism: Argument in the Disciplines* (Buckingham: Open University Press, 1992), p.4.

[2] David Jones, *Dai Greatcoat: A Self-Portrait in his Letters* (London: Faber & Faber, 1980), pp.98 and 106.

[3] René Hague, *A Commentary on The Anathemata of David Jones* (Wellingborough: Christopher Skelton, 1977), p.38.

[4] Deborah Thom, 'A Lop-sided View: Feminist History or the History of Women?', in Campbell, *Critical Feminism*, p.49.

[5] Lynda Nead, *The Female Nude: Art, Obscenity and Sexuality* (London: Routledge, 1992), p.8.

[6] J. Williams, *The Psychology of Women* (London: Norton, 1987), p.1.

[7] Jeremy Hooker, *David Jones: An Exploratory Study* (London: Enitharmon, 1975), p.27.

[8] Toril Moi, 'Men in Feminism', in Campbell, *Critical Feminism*, p.39.

[9] Paul Hills, *David Jones* (London: Tate Gallery, 1981), p.58.

[10] Jessie Weston, *From Ritual to Romance* (New York: Doubleday, 1957), p.75.

[11] Hague, *Commentary*, p.38.

[12] Luke 2:35.

[13] Virginia Woolf, 'Women and Fiction', in Michele Barrett (ed.), *Virginia Woolf: Women and Writing* (London: The Women's Press, 1979), p.48.

[14] Ibid., p.48.

[15] Virginia Woolf, 'Dorothy Richardson', in Barrett, *Virginia Woolf*, p.191.

[16] Janet Wolff, *Feminine Sentences: Essays on Women and Culture* (Cambridge: Polity Press, 1990), pp.82–3.

[17] Margaret Iversen, 'Mary Kelly and Grizelda Pollock in Conversation', in Campbell, *Critical Feminism*, p.184.

[18] Marshall Berman, *All that is Solid Melts into Air: The Experience of Modernity* (London: Verso, 1983), p.137.

David Jones:
Making Space for the Warring Factions

DEREK SHIEL

As a boy of eight David Jones made a drawing which he always kept by him and, somewhat surprisingly, would say to visitors late in life that it was still his favourite. The drawing, of a dancing bear, has been reproduced in more than one book of his paintings as well as appearing in several exhibitions. Certainly it shows uncommon talent. The bear is seen from the side, standing erect with paws extended, the creature's outline delicately varied in emphasis, the fur indicated by little tufts across its body in a way that can be recognized many years afterwards in Jones's mature work. The beast is muzzled but must also have worn a collar and chain; its keeper would have carried a long staff to restrain it, the end of which is just visible on the left upper edge of the composition. In studying this early drawing we have two options: we can see it as that of a child, of exceptional quality, or choose to go further and consider it to have meaning as an expressive image. Did Jones, I wonder, when older sense that the drawing possessed a richer connotation, greater validity, as he would say, as a *sign*? But if so, a sign of what? The animal does, in fact, reappear in *Trystan ac Essyllt*, one of his last two painted drawings, each of them filled with significant references.[1]

On a pennant, in the same erect position, the bear flies aloft from an unseen mast, aboard the ship on which Trystan and Essyllt make their fateful voyage. This time the beast is without a muzzle, placed in juxta-position to part of the constellation of the Great Bear, Arcturus; Arcturus puts us in mind of Arthur, the once and future king, one of whose knights, Lancelot, turned him into a cuckold. Here King Mark is almost being turned into one through his emissary Trystan's calamitous passion for Mark's bride-to-be. These two stories speak of an Oedipal conflict with kingship. The bear on the pennant tilts slightly backwards, an uncomfortable or unwilling witness to the drama unfolding in front of it where, against the configuration of stars, a vividly red, serpentine dragon writhes its way across the night sky towards the bear. While red is heraldically accurate, is the colour not apt in more ways than one, the colour of blood, of passion, of Luciferian fire streaked across the heavens? Why, I ask, should the bear be the snake's quarry? Here, possibly, is Blake's worm made visible.[2]

By comparison, the childhood bear is shown in a simple context of fence and pavement, dumb witness to what it cannot comprehend, apparently docile yet with potentially vicious claws. What is evident is the boy's sensitivity to the creature's nature and circumstance. From the side this bear on hind legs appears noble rather than ferocious, devoid of astrological or totemic significance. It is a sympathetic depiction of an animal, partially tamed, subjected to an existence in suburban surroundings, disciplined to remain upright to please others. Could there not have been an identification on the part of an imaginative child with this creature's plight? In placing the second bear in a scene of amorous confusion does Jones unwittingly allude to his own unconscious boyhood conflict with his father, having as he did to share a bedroom with his parents, until at least the age of five?[3]

A performing bear, as already mentioned, is muzzled; it has been collared, chained (Aphrodite in Jones's much later picture *Aphrodite in Aulis* is also chained, but at the ankle), the staff or rod its keeper carries is used as a scourge, rather than being a source of comfort as in the twenty-third Psalm, and most crucially the bear dances to another's tune, having, as William Blissett writes in his essay 'The Scapebeast', 'become servile, thwarted of its nature', its untamed, wild state. Could it be said of Jones that at times he too was unable to dance to his own tune, whether he realized it or not?

It was also in his childhood that Jones first began to draw animals at the zoo. That he later became fully aware of their captive state, although depicting them on paper as free, is made plain in lines from 'The Book of Balaam's Ass':

> ... like when pale flanks turn to lace with agile stripes the separating
> grill – until you quite forget the necessary impertinence
> the shackling and iron security
> by which and
> in which and
> through which
> you indulge your fine appreciation. (*RQ*, 187)

Jones is being ironical here, maybe about matters other than the observation of an animal. Curiously, his words could almost as well describe a visitor's encounter with the religious of an enclosed Order, spoken to through an iron grille and admired for their sanctity. Possibly 'fine appreciation' also refers to his own practice as a fine artist of making drawings of caged animals, for the time being forgetting 'the necessary impertinence' of his action. Another much more poignant reading of these ambiguous lines, which in the poem immediately and abruptly follow an appreciation of Lady Prudence Pelham, a woman he greatly loved, could suggest that he must of necessity view her from an emotionally caged state, which would be a discreet way of indicating why their relationship was never more than platonic. Moving further back in time, could these lines even refer to a shadowy memory of watching his mother through the bars of his cot near her bedside, wearing her nightgown trimmed with lace?[4]

In case such observations appear far-fetched or crude, I will quote from Jones's Preface to his second long poem, *The Anathemata*:

> The arts abhor any loppings off of meanings or emptying out, any lessening of the totality of connotation, any loss of recession or thickness through. (*A*, 24)

In itself this statement by an artist seems well and good, but I need to follow it by another from the same source with which it could be at variance:

> Moreover, the workman must be dead to himself while engaged upon the work, otherwise we have that sort of 'self-expression' which is as undesirable in the painter or writer as in the carpenter, the cantor, the half-back or the cook. (*A*, 12)[5]

In the act of creation a necessary mortification must apparently take place *whatever* type of maker is involved. As a painter, sculptor and writer myself, I prefer to suggest the reverse: that artists in this century, after the fracturing of the western cultural tradition, have often had to open up to themselves in whatever ways they have been capable of, that these ways may be what take them into and beyond themselves, and that such journeys can be terrifying to any artist who must undergo them, ordeals that perhaps cannot be avoided. By 1952, when *The Anathemata* was published, Jones believed that it was necessary to deaden himself, whereas I suggest, admittedly with hindsight, that he did so at his peril and for specific and paradoxical reasons. Self-expression may be undesirable but, none the less, it is at times not merely necessary but essential to the well-being and development of an artist. Let me be more explicit: the deadening Jones writes of very probably served him well as poet but played havoc with the painter in him, an intuitive painter whose material was mined in a different, and for Jones potentially catastrophic, way.[6] The painter who is dead to himself may in fact be attempting to

lop off meaning, to empty out, to permit less than the totality of connotation, that is, only what he can safely and sanely accommodate. Choices
become stark, but to make a choice is not necessarily to resolve; it can
often be no more than a temporary solution.

Many people do not know that Jones suffered several nervous breakdowns; two short bouts of collapse in the 1920s were followed by much
more profound illnesses in 1932 and 1947. The reason for such general
ignorance is simple: most writing on his painting or poetry says little
about these collapses.[7] In the breakdown of 1932 something momentous
and terrifying surfaced which was adversely to affect his subsequent
work as a painter. Once this has been grasped Jones's whole œuvre is
understood differently and, as a consequence, if we value his arts and his
life, each becomes more astonishing, more poignant, more awesome: the
arts more astonishing in their amount, their range and content, the life
more poignant because of the suffering involved, more awesomely
courageous and celebratory. Paradoxically, in his failure lay something
he would come to see as success: he was almost never again able to paint
as freely or joyfully as before but was enabled to make of himself a poet
of genius and an excellent essayist and to place himself amongst the
finest of European calligraphers through the making of his painted
inscriptions.

By 1932 Jones had become completely the artist; having laid aside
engraving and carving he was, it appeared, fully concentrated on his
primary vocation – as a painter. His membership of the Seven and Five
Society, a group of explorative young painters and sculptors, which
included Ben and Winifred Nicholson, Christopher Wood, Ivon
Hitchens, Henry Moore and Barbara Hepworth, had not only encouraged
him to paint more frequently in oils but had also provoked a greater
openness towards what a painting might now be.

In this year he managed to make a considerable number of watercolours and, while they vary in subject matter and in the ways they are
painted, one group of table tops with objects is particularly worth
mentioning. Jones's method had been to sketch quickly in pencil before
applying watercolour and this initial drawing might be added to in the
process of painting. Indeed it was frequently the drawing which held the
work together, providing both armature and emphasis for the end result.
In the group of still lifes on tablecloths the whole page is flooded with
watercolour, and at first, using a big brush, large floating areas are
created into which the objects, few in number, are placed in loose,
blobbed or scribbled paint. No preliminary drawing is felt necessary in
this ocean of pigment. Jones was liberating himself, swimming away
from the safety of shore, no markers discernible in the open sea. In

some of these pictures the surface becomes the arena, descriptions of perspective no more than alluded to. He is, at last, fully a modern painter in his use of space and now a master of brushwork: subject matter and paint are unified.

Just then it was that Jones suffered his first major breakdown. I have said that he appeared to be fully concentrated on his vocation as a painter. But he had, in addition, almost finished *In Parenthesis*, his first long poem, although it was not to be completed until several years later and finally published in 1937. What was momentous was that he had become a poet; what was immensely to be regretted was the impact this had on his development as a painter and as a man. Jones had experienced warfare as a soldier and relived it in the writing of *In Parenthesis*; as a result war had become horrendously, insidiously internalized for he found himself faced by contradictory imperatives: as poet he needed to gain greater knowledge in diverse areas of learning; whereas he needed to lay aside a burden of knowledge acquired as a painter, if he was to explore further the new kind of space he had discovered through an increasingly spontaneous method of working. How could requirements so opposed be reconciled?

Jones felt the profoundest need to become whole as a creator – by means of the arts he practised.[8] We now know that he is an artist who finds his stature in shaping each facet of himself, rather than by pursuing one art single-mindedly while ignoring the possibility of attempting any other (as, say, Matthew Smith, Soutine or Bacon). That being so, I wonder if Jones's first breakdown was the result of reaching out towards an expansion of his individual creative nature, through developing into a poet, and *simultaneously* finding himself, as a visionary Christian painter, moving nearer the void of the essential nature of being? Particularly for an artist, could these goals not actually be one: the discovery of one's own true nature as an integral part of the essence of being? Perhaps – but such a goal would have been well-nigh impossible for a committed Christian of that period. As viewed from the perspective of the Roman Catholic Church in the 1930s, I am told that to seek out one's true nature or to pursue the essential nature of being would have been considered far from one and the same and, most probably, neither would have been deemed advisable or particularly welcomed.

Christianity makes great demands on its adherents, in part because of its spiritual goals, in part through traditional devotional observance. Here already division can occur as many mystics have discovered, finding themselves in conflict with their religious superiors as they travel a spiritual path. The true nature of being may have one meaning for a highly developed religious mind but quite another in the experience of a spiritual and creative heart; St John of the Cross, for one, makes this dichotomy clear. Love, Eros or Agape, affairs, cohabitation, marriage or celibacy can be a cause of division within the self,[9] as is warfare, waged by Christians but altogether incompatible with the teachings of Christ. For the Christian artist any or all of these issues may become crucial concerns, and there is yet another division to be wrestled with, that between the way of beauty and the way of goodness, between the dictates of art and morality – whether to choose consecration to beauty or renunciation of the self and its desires.[10] Gerard Manley Hopkins, one of the poets Jones most admired, is an example in his art and life of the physical, emotional, sexual and aesthetic torment such questions can engender, in his case exacerbated by his double vocation as poet and priest.[11]

In Jones's quest he happened upon treble lines of defence: first, his own and others' predictable inclination to avoid the depths of introspection and, secondly, the barrier of Church doctrine which instructed him in what he should believe, must do and not do, over against whatever he might intuitively, needily discover for himself or see happening around him, for instance in the emotional and sexual explorations among his Catholic friends and acquaintances. As a convert, and being who he was, he wanted to get things right, to behave as he ought as a moral being. The third line of defence encountered by him in this first breakdown and to a lesser extent in the second was that his doctors or psychiatrists, to say the very least, were not as versed in or attentive to spiritual teaching or artistic exploration as he was. Thus his bafflement and anger grew, and under the strain of his essentially spiritual dilemma he crumpled. In this collapse it is easy to see retreat into emotional neediness, but was there not also beneath his scarcely voiced cry for help, the cry he could like Soutine or Munch not really utter, a deeper desire to be reborn into life renewed and integrated before attaining middle age? In his groping towards mysticism, evident in sentences slipped into letters and quickly qualified or disavowed, he was split between alternatives of self and self-lessness, between polarities, wanting on the one hand to let go of the bodily, the embodied, the tactile, as is observable in the watercolours I have mentioned, and on the other desiring to become fully incarnate through sexual love, rather than remain separated, as can be glimpsed in his tentative advances towards and away from women, these too avowed and disavowed to friends. Once he had become a poet could the Word become flesh or in painting could it dissolve into this new space he was discovering alongside other artists, a space of pure being, white, emptied out – but far from being without meaning?

This has been the problem of much painting in this century, how real or how fragmented, how abstract or sublime, to make it; in different ways Klee and Picasso are examples and we need to put Jones fairly and squarely in this larger western context. Most painters, however, have sexual lives, even most abstract painters. For Jones the emerging drama of figurative or abstract, the disembodied, took on a far more knife-edged intensity, psychologically, spiritually and creatively, for now he had become poet as well as painter. He was no longer muzzled but would he allow himself to speak of his personal troubles? All his warring factions were now in place and would harry him for the rest of his life.

From 'The Book of Balaam's Ass' again:

(for space itself, they say, leans, is kindly, with ourselves, who make wide deviations to meet ourselves). (*RQ*, 188)

The 'wide deviation' of becoming a poet he could attain but the deviation of greater freedom as a painter he could not because, in all probability, he sensed it might prove far from 'kindly'.[12] Elsewhere, with Jonathan Miles, I have written of the curious affinity between the ideas of certain American Abstract Expressionist painters and those of Jones in the 1940s.[13] Their dedicated articulation of a new space was to prove hazardous in the extreme, leading many of them to an untimely death from alcoholism, accident, suicide or cancer.

I must return to Christian teaching in mentioning Jones's preoccupation with the Mass; 'the Mass makes sense of everything', he would say, quoting Jacques Maritain.[14] The danger, I suggest, in constant memorial of the death of Christ on the Cross is to remain with the sacrifice and not move to resurrection, either of the body or of the spirit. Maritain counsels: 'the artist is subject to a kind of asceticism which may at times demand heroic sacrifice.'[15] Did this symbolic, religious or ritual fixation on the Mass by Maritain or Maurice de la Taille, with which Jones eagerly complied, hamper his spiritual, and in turn his painterly, development, and was it eventually even a toxic ingredient in his own bodily and emotional suffering, as a man, as believer, as painter although not as seriously as poet? What was bitter for Jones, poignant and awesome surely for us, was the fact that what propelled him into his first breakdown left him spiritually defeated.[16] He failed in his, perhaps partially conscious, attempt to attain the state when, as Blake says, 'the doors of perception are cleansed' or, as the Buddhists describe it, there is a 'turning around at the seat of consciousness'. In Jones's quoting of Mandeville in his Preface to *In Parenthesis* in 1937, I cannot but hear the undertones of a far more personal lament: 'Of Paradys ne can I not speken propurly, I was not there; it is fer beyonde and that for thinketh me. And also I was not worthi.'[17]

Jones returned to life, having been unable to 'empty himself out', to escape the cage, the chain or the rod, and instead, by degrees, made for himself and for us 'a heap of all that he could find'.[18] He bore bravely within himself the warring factions of his manhood, of his beliefs, of being both painter and poet continually trying, dedicated infantryman that he was, to give these factions shape and meaning. Nevertheless I no longer favour such a neat conclusion; in this essay I have only been able to explore one artist's relation to illness, but I believe much more remains to be understood about the maladies of certain nineteenth- and twentieth-century painters and writers, when studied in the context of their society, and when their place within it is more precisely defined. Were Jones, for instance, to be viewed in relation to the roles of either mystic or shaman, his breakdowns would have to be thought of quite differently, not as due to the vulnerability of a sensitive, shell-shocked war veteran but either as dark nights of the soul or the ordeals necessary in the making of a shaman.[19]

The practice of several arts demands of the artist an ability to shift attention, to alter and readjust his mental states, to differentiate. Each art will elicit varied features of his or her nature as the artist discovers what it is possible to achieve in that particular art form, what is inherent in its process and what he or she is able to express through its means. We marvel at the multiple talent of Michelangelo, draughtsman, painter, sculptor, architect and poet, or in our century Picasso, equally talented, but following a different path. Michelangelo seeks to dedicate his work to the greater glory of God whereas Picasso makes plain that he does not seek, he finds: he creates and transforms from sheer delight and the urgency of his need to do so. Jones would seem to be part of each of these possibilities: his work is made as an expression of his love for his Creator, but his relationship to his adopted religion and role as an artist in the culture of twentieth-century western society differs greatly from Michelangelo's to Catholicism or his participation in the Italian Renaissance. Jones, somewhat like Picasso, is drawn back towards man's earliest acts of creation, the Lascaux caves, the Willendorf Venus, the first implements of bone, but Jones cannot ignore what he senses as the essentially spiritual function underlying his making, constituting a sacramental act.

A small drawing by him shows a man who wears the head and antlers of a deer standing in front of a group of trees. Along the forest floor in front of him runs the spiral of a trough dug into the ground, a primitive image of a labyrinth. Maybe it was a sketch for an illustration of one of his poems. The image seems to me the result of his being all that he was as a creator, but here is a unity that he did not live to experience where the figure he depicts is both maker and spiritual guide, about to lead or participate in a ritual act on sacred ground for the well-being of his community, an act involving the deployment of many arts. This journey, back or forward in time towards a shamanic figure, a combination probably of artist, healer and priest, is, I suggest, the one Jones found himself intuitively pursuing, where all his warring factions would become fused into wholeness.

Notes

[1] For *Trystan ac Essyllt* see *David Jones*, exhibition catalogue (London: Tate Gallery, 1981), p.125. For *Dancing Bear* and *Aphrodite in Aulis* see fig. 1 and the frontispiece to this book.

[2] See William Blake's poem: 'O Rose, thou art sick!'

[3] See 'In illo tempore', in *The Dying Gaul*, p.19. For Jones's identification with both Lancelot and Trystan see Colin Wilcockson's detailed essay in H. Erskine-Hill and R. A. McCabe (eds.), *Presenting Poetry* (Cambridge: Cambridge University Press, 1995), pp.235–56, and remarks of Arthur Giardelli in his essay 'Trystan ac Essyllt by David Jones', *Agenda*, 11, 4 and 12, 1 (1973/4), 52.

[4] There are very many sketches and several paintings by David Jones of young women wearing a flimsy type of nightdress.

[5] On arrival at Ditchling, Jones was initially advised to try carpentry but before long was considered inept; he acted occasionally as cantor for the Offices, was later a cook but as seldom as possible and never a half-back. In his role of poet, however, he was both 'carpenter of song' and, in declaiming his work, a sort of cantor. Self-expression, surely, would have a different connotation for each of these workmen; how it may be utilized in diverse professions seems to me a worthwhile question. In the writing of a sort of epic poetry Jones is not, of course, alone in advocating an impersonal voice; T. S. Eliot, for instance, does the same. However, I contend that Jones's stance as a painter is far from being impersonal, hence his breakdowns relate more to painting than poetry.

[6] See Nicolete Gray, *The Paintings of David Jones* (London: Lund Humphries, 1989), pp.41, 49, for descriptions of the alteration in Jones's manner of working on a painting as a result of his breakdown in 1932. Those who admire and quote his emphatic statement about self-expression ignore the complexity of Jones's own predicament as a painter, understandably, since so does he in making it.

[7] I am indebted to Prof. Thomas Dilworth for information about the first two bouts of illness in the 1920s.

[8] See the essay 'Art and Sacrament' (1955) reprinted in *Epoch and Artist*, p.153. The entire essay relates to my theme of warring factions as it details the problems involved for Jones in 'a consideration of the nature of Ars'.

[9] See Octavio Paz, *The Double Flame*, tr. Helen Lane (London: Harvill Press, 1996), a series of essays on love and eroticism.

[10] For much of what I write about mysticism and the Roman Catholic Church I am indebted to Fr Anthony Meredith SJ who explained: 'For the mystic journey one

needs to lean on an insightful and trustworthy father confessor as guide – he holds the knowledge, shapes the journey as one surrenders into being.' Jones turned to psychoanalysis because for a layman such a monk or priest may be impossible to find.

[11] See *Poems and Prose of Gerard Manley Hopkins*, Introduction by W. H. Gardner (Harmondsworth: Penguin, 1953), where the torment of Hopkins is simply described.

[12] See Jones's quotation from *The Mabinogion*: 'Evil betide me etc.,' at the beginning of *In Parenthesis*. Jones opened the door and subsequently attempted to close it, but it would not remain shut.

[13] Jonathan Miles and Derek Shiel, *David Jones: The Maker Unmade* (Bridgend: Seren, 1995), p.237.

[14] Jacques Maritain, *The Philosophy of Art*, tr. Fr John O'Connor (Ditchling: St Dominic's Press, 1923), p.22.

[15] Maritain, *Philosophy of Art*, p.41.

[16] See *David Jones: Ten Letters*, ed. Derek Shiel (London: Agenda Editions, 1996), pp.30, 38, for comments by Jones about his breakdowns and his art.

[17] See the Preface to *In Parenthesis*, p.xiii. For a passionate diagnosis of the western attachment to the way of struggle, the strife of Lucifer, see E. M. Cioran's essay 'Thinking against Oneself', in *The Temptation to Exist*, tr. Richard Howard (London: Quartet Books, 1987), pp.33–47.

[18] See the Preface to *The Anathemata*, p.9.

[19] See Michael Tucker, *Dreaming with Open Eyes* (San Francisco: Aquarian Harper, 1992), a study of the shamanic spirit in relation to twentieth-century art and culture; Jones is unmentioned but deserves a place.

David Jones and The Ancient Mariner: Diversity in Unity

BELINDA HUMFREY

> Slung so, it swings its full weight. With you going blindly on all paws, it slews its whole length, to hang at your bowed neck like the Mariner's white oblation. (*In Parenthesis*, 184)

The simile here gives powerful visual force to David Jones's description of a First World War soldier burdened by his rifle. The 'Mariner's white oblation' is, of course, the giant bird, the albatross of Coleridge's *The Rime of the Ancient Mariner* which his fellow mariners (supposedly) hung about the Mariner's neck, in punishment or reminder, when evil fell upon their ship after he with his 'cross-bow . . . shot the Albatross':

> Instead of the cross, the Albatross
> About my neck was hung. (II, 414–2)[1]

The hanging albatross provides a visual image of great weight; but why does Jones describe it as the Mariner's 'oblation'? 'Oblation' suggests an offering, a sacrifice to gods or God, more precisely in Church terms (significant for the Roman Catholic Jones) the offerings of bread and wine in the Eucharist (for post-Reformation Roman Catholics, the Mass), themselves representative of the body and blood of Christ. By no reasonable means can the albatross in Coleridge's poem be seen to represent any of these. It is a 'bird', a fellow being of the natural universe, which should have been loved with all other beings, 'man and bird and beast' (as the all too simple moral at the end of the *Rime* dictates (612–14)), but is killed for no apparent reason; it had been welcomed and fed by the ship's crew 'As if it had been a Christian soul' (65) (possibly a reference to the belief of sailors that albatrosses carried the souls of dead sailors). Jones's interpretation of *The Ancient Mariner* here appears to be askew. In this study I shall consider David Jones's creative oddity in his reading of Coleridge's long poem.

The Ancient Mariner was a work which Jones had 'enjoyed from childhood' (*DG*, 186). Early in 1929, he completed ten copper-plate engravings as illustrations to the poem, at the request of the young Bristol publisher, Douglas Cleverdon. It was in the year 1928, when he was working at these engravings – and he recalled that he made 150–200 drawings for the ten plates – that Jones began to write *In Parenthesis* (1937). It was not until 1964 that he wrote 'An Introduction to *The Rime of the Ancient Mariner*', an essay of some forty pages intended to accompany a reproduction of the illustrations. (Because of its length, it was delayed in publication until 1972.)[2] Meantime, Jones had produced *The Anathemata* (1952) which, more than *In Parenthesis*, is coloured by his reading of *The Ancient Mariner*, such as is revealed in those much earlier copper-engravings and the later essay, in addition to its unmissable scattering of small quotations or echoes from the poem.

In his 'Introduction' of 1964, both before and after embarking on a confident exposition and interpretation of Coleridge's poem, Jones makes some sort of apology for the quality of his illustrations. At the beginning, this apology is offered mainly for the quality of the craftsmanship. He explains that in 1928 he was only a 'novice' in copper-plate engraving, although 'fairly efficient as an engraver on wood'; hence, he decided 'nothing elaborate should be attempted' (*DG*, 187). The brilliantly memorable wood-engravings of Jones's several illustrative series of the 1920s, *Gulliver's Travels*, *The Book of Jonah* and *The Chester Book of the Deluge*, make dramatic use of black and white spaces (in fact with sophisticated play on significant areas of white, such as the white angel and Jonah contrasting with the (black) evil city of Nineveh, or Jonah whiter than the sailors who seize him); they are probably more appealing aesthetically than the linear designs of the *Ancient Mariner* plates which one must scrutinize closely and slowly in order to discover their patterns and detail. The most immediately visually attractive of the eight main plates for *The Mariner* is *The Death Fires* (Plate iii) because the black cross-hatch of the ship and masts stands out; whereas this is visually and conceptually the least adventurous of the series.

> I decided that simple incised lines, reinforced here and there as sparingly as possible by cross-hatched areas (e.g. the hull, masts, yard and spars of the stricken ship in the third full-page illustration), was the only way open to me. I decided also that these essentially linear designs should have an undertone over the whole area of the plate, partly as an aid to unification. This is easily and naturally achieved in copper-plate printing by not wiping the plate totally clean of ink before putting it in the press. (*DG*, 187)

Where a rejected drawing for one of the *Mariner* copper-engravings has survived, it is interesting to see Jones struggling not so much for unification in lines but unification in the overall design itself. The later improved drawing for Plate viii, showing fisher-folk arriving to attend Vespers, has its figures all pushed to the edges of the frame, an amazing blank space at their centre.[3] It is as though the prospect of engraving copper defeated the brilliant designer of the *Chester Deluge* (1927). Wood-engravings do not require such devices as an unwiped plate for unification; the organization of black, white and grey to give 'unity' was however a skill Jones admired in Bewick.[4] Jones's ingenious illustrations of *Gulliver's Travels* depend for their impact on the restricted space apparently imposed by their frames, especially when they play amusingly on relative sizes; all Jones has to do as illustrator is use Dr Johnson's reduction of Swift's satire: 'Big men and little men and there you have it all.' Certain of the *Jonah* plates suggest a story-line similar to the *Ancient Mariner*'s: a stricken ship and a crew threatening a central figure, as sailors draw lots for their scapegoat, and then seize Jonah: they convey vividly the feel of the physical threat and fear possible in human society. There is plenty that is physical in the voyage of Coleridge's Ancient Mariner, the anger of the crew, their dying of drought, the curse in their dead eyes, being only a beginning. But the poem also describes the *spiritual* journey of the Mariner, generally read as some form of sin, punishment and partial redemption, out at sea, in a world of natural and supernatural spirits. It is surprising that Jones does not argue that copper-engraving, productive of a multiplicity of fine lines on a white background, is appropriate to convey insubstantial, spiritual experience. What Jones does say, with emphatic repetition, is that copper-engraving for him 'precluded cleverness and any attempt at complexity'. He comforts himself that there is some parallel or match between Coleridge's surface-art in his ballad-tale:

it has a deceptive surface ease and facility and a simplicity of artistry, so that the rapid and easy flow of its versification makes it read as if it were written without effort, (*DG*, 189)

and the simple 'linear freedom and firmness' possible in metal engraving:

I am of the opinion that the most specific beauty, that which belongs to copper-engraving, *sui generis*, is a lyricism inherent in the clean, furrowed free, fluent engraved line, as quintessentially linear as the painted lines . . . in Botticelli's . . . illustrations to the *Divina Commedia* or the purely linear designs in Anglo-Saxon illustrated MSS. (*DG*, 188)

In describing the movement of the 'steel burin on the resistant copper', he is using, appropriately, Coleridge's line on ship-movement: 'The furrow follow'd free' (*DG*, 187).

Given that there are advantages together with disadvantages in his method of illustrating *The Ancient Mariner*, Jones acknowledges a deficiency in his treatment of the poem's content. His problem is that Coleridge's poem of surface simplicity is a 'great creative' work of much complexity, 'layer-upon layer of meaning' (*DG*, 189). He further notes 'the elusive quality of the poem', 'its deep allusions' and its 'imagery' of 'metamorphic quality', saying that there is something of the Welsh *hud a lledrith* in the poem, meaning 'magic and illusion' (*DG*, 190). Thus it is, apparently, that in the penultimate paragraph of his 'Introduction' Jones writes of the 'poverty' of his engravings 'compared with the great riches of the poem they attempted to illustrate'. Possibly some of this realization of the engravings' 'poverty' in content came to the older David Jones, although the theme which he extracts from, or imposes on *The Ancient Mariner* in 1928–9 is one which he carried into the 1950s.

This theme is indicated early in the 1964 'Introduction':

> In that it has a bearing on my approach to *The Mariner* and hence on something in my illustrations, I would like to quote in shortened form a note to a passage in my book *The Anathemata* in which seafarers in peril use the suffrage 'Count us among his argonauts whose argosy you plead'. To this passage I appended a note somewhat to the following effect: What is pleaded in the Mass is precisely the argosy or voyage of the Redeemer, his entire sufferings, death, resurrection and ascension. It is this that is offered on behalf of us argonauts and the whole argosy of mankind and indeed in some sense of all earthly creation, which, as Paul says, suffers a common travail.

This was written about 1950, but a couple of decades previously when Jones was working on the *Mariner* engravings associations of a like nature were already an influence, though less explicit. (*DG*, 190)

Much of the 'Introduction to *The Ancient Mariner*' is about the 'Celtic tales of wonder-voyages' to the northern regions, 'early Christian images of the ship, the mast, the ordeals', what he calls 'the Christus-Ulysses concept' which he says defiantly to his reader again, at the end of the essay, 'have a bearing on Coleridge's poem, because ... the poem cannot escape evoking the whole argosy of man' (*DG*, 223).

Here seems to be a selective (and dubious) interpretation of *The*

Ancient Mariner which Jones believes is reflected in his illustrations. However, his 'Introduction', while selective of some of his obsessions, finds him working carefully through Coleridge's story in the poem, noting its riches and certainly getting its outline right. Here is one summarizing part:

> There is the voyaging, the terrible and mysterious hazards, the offence that must be purged, the loosening of the spell by an interior act of love, when the Mariner, observing the iridescent beauty of the water-snakes, 'blessed them unaware' ... That act of praise is, I suppose, the crux of the poem. (*DG*, 193)

With some obvious omissions, Jones's illustrations do provide a fairly literal representation of the poem's story. Of Jones's ten illustrations, eight are full-page (figs. 13 and 14). They are preceded by a head-piece sketch of a ship in full sail leaving a harbour. They are finished by a tail-piece sketch of a pelican feeding her young from her own breast – often emblematic of Christ or the Church – with a Latin inscription which Jones translates, 'May the Lord kindle in us the fire of his love and the flame of his charity'; he relates it to *The Ancient Mariner*'s late moral that we should love 'man and bird and beast' (*DG*, 225).

Plate i, *The Wedding Guests*, is full of movement. The bride, with flowing robes, sweeps upwards into a hall of classical architecture by the seashore, followed by elegant youths in medieval dress carrying flowers and hats of flowing feathers, while, forefront, the aged, bearded mariner seizes a young and frightened guest, his skinny hands coming through the stair rail.

Plate ii, *The Albatross*, is also dramatic and imaginative because we are given a sky-view of the albatross, apparently struck in full flight and pinned to the top cross-bar of a mast, while at its base four minute, circled sailor-figures throw up their arms in horror. At the forefront and on a diagonal horizon are icebergs in a crackling, howling sea.

Plate iii, *The Death-Fires*, shows almost the whole of a ship with sagging sails with which a crowd of sailors are struggling, again with arms raised high. On the horizon are both the fiery sun and the moon and stars which revolve through the days and nights of the Mariner's agony. In the foreground are nine comparatively very large and long-tailed lizard-like sea-creatures, the 'slimy things' of the poem.

Plate iv, *Life-in-Death*, brings a close-up of the crew of the spectre-ship hailed by the parched Mariner. Death, a skeleton, and Life-in-Death, a slender prostitute (dressed as if for the Folies Bergère), make a circle (like Fortune's wheel) with their raised, dicing arms and

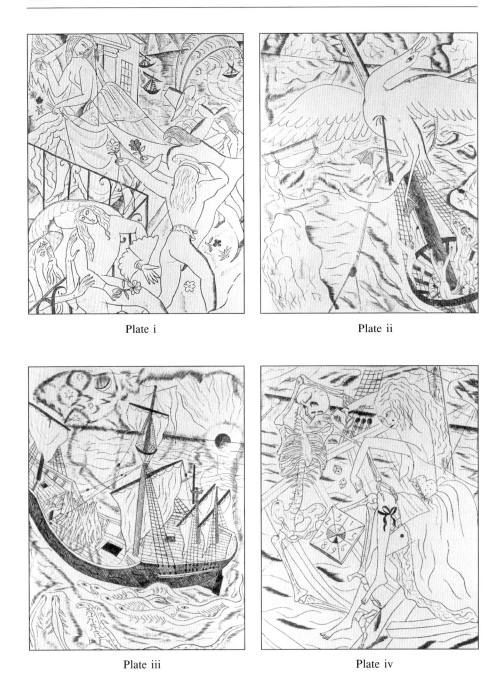

Plate i   Plate ii

Plate iii   Plate iv

Fig. 13: David Jones, *The Rime of the Ancient Mariner*, copper engravings i–iv

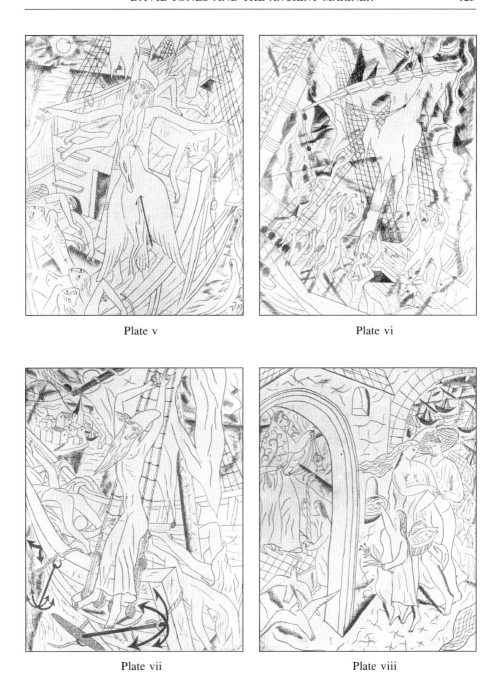

Plate v

Plate vi

Plate vii

Plate viii

Fig. 14: David Jones, *The Rime of the Ancient Mariner*, copper engravings v–viii

their crossed legs. They seem to float between the bare spars of their ship like the falling dice which are to decide the fate of the Mariner and crew.

These are varied and imaginative plates, aesthetically, given their simplicity of form and style. In the next three plates we move onto the Mariner's ship and have to find the figures among much hull, deck, rigging, etc.

Plate v, *The Curse*, has at its centre the Mariner standing on deck, dressed in an Anglo-Saxon manuscript-style cap and robe, his long bearded head bowed, his arms and hands outstretched horizontally without support – in a crucified position; unrealistically hung from his neck by a string round its neck is the dead albatross, of equivalent body-length, its head bowed in unison with the Mariner's, its side still pierced, this suggesting some form of joint crucifixion. Around the Mariner on the deck lie young naked bodies, their eyes turned to the Mariner. Watersnakes and lizards swim by.

Plate vi, *The Mariners*, focuses on masts and rigging as the 'ghastly crew' of lifeless but resurrected sailors 'work the ropes' of the ship which moves without a breeze. Some are in the rigging, but some beneath a ragged sail seem to be doing a hornpipe with raised arms, rather than anything functional. Waves of shadow and misty cross-hatching convey the 'ghastly' horror.

Plate vii, *The Town*, is possibly too close in design to Plate v with which it is intended to contrast. The same emaciated Mariner, now without the Albatross, stands stretched out against the rigging which is fastened to the outside of the ship's hull. (This is one of many details which suggest that Jones was aware of Gustave Doré's engraved illustrations to *The Mariner*.) One of the Mariner's raised arms provides a priestly blessing (which seems inappropriate for his situation). Some of the dead crew again lie upon the deck but with their heads, and thus their eyes, out of view. To the front are a couple of anchors, suggesting land and haven. The fishing town of the title – a medieval-style sketch – is in the distance.

Plate viii, *Vespers*, obviously takes up the captured Wedding Guest's protest,

> The wedding guests are there:
>
> . . .
> And hark the little vesper bell,
> Which biddeth me to prayer! (VII, 592–6)

and shows, as Jones says in his 'Introduction', 'the sea-faring folk of the little port' ascending to Vespers in a church of Romanesque architecture. At their front is a family with a plainly dressed mother and daughter – contrasting with the two actual women of the poem, the bride and the courtesan Life-in-Death. The fisher-folk carry a basket of fish, an oblation emblematic of Christ.

This plate is the one which Jones feels demands an explanation in his 'Introduction', obviously because it contains figures and details not in the poem, especially the priest censing an altar:

> It is at Vespers that the altar is censed during the singing of the Magnificat, her song who is called the Star of the Sea. (*DG*, 225)

At the end of his illustrations, if it is not, as he liked to quote from Maritain, 'The Mass [which] makes sense of everything',[5] then it is a gentler church service with reference to 'Mary Mother'. But in fact Jones has enlarged the Vespers plate into an interpretation as the Mass, with his 'tail-piece' plate. The inscription on this 'is taken from the Roman Mass, the words being part of what the celebrant says while he is censing the altar after having censed the Oblations' (*DG*, 225). In addition to this, the intervention of 'the Mother of God' as extension and opposition to Life-in-Death's activities is an event Jones reads inventively into the poem in his 'Introduction'. His evidence comes from the Mariner's (simple and only) exclamation,

> To Mary Queen the praise be given!
> She sent the gentle rain from Heaven
> That slid into my soul. (V, 294–6)

together with Coleridge's late-added gloss (his glosses, I would argue, being for him another fictional, 'medieval' frill and not his own explanation): 'By grace of the holy Mother, the ancient Mariner is refreshed with rain.'

> [T]he Mother of God lulls him for a while in slumber, *as in a kind of Pietà*, and while he slumbers *she invokes the heavens* to refresh him with gentle rain. (*DG*, 198, my italics)

Jones goes on to say,

> *The Crux-cry, 'I thirst'*, that for 'seven days, seven nights' had been his unvoiced cry ... was now ... given effectual response. (*DG*, 198, my italics)

It is puzzling that Jones does not also therefore describe as a 'Crux-cry'
the Mariner's lines to the Wedding Guest:

> this soul hath been
> Alone on a wide wide sea:
> So lonely 'twas, that God himself
> Scarce seemèd there to be. (VII, 596–600)

But, despite his suggestions in the engravings and the 'Introduction',
apparently Jones knows that the Mariner is not Christ the Redeemer, nor
a Christian here imitating Christ. He does not develop the idea further,
although he suggests in Plates iv and v of his engravings that the
Albatross may be identified with the crucified Christ. (Jones's suggestion
of this identification may be seen by contrasting his image of the shot
albatross with those of Doré (1876) and Mervyn Peake (1943, Peake's
indian ink and wash illustrations, like Jones's, owing much to Doré's
designs). Doré and Peake both depict the bird shot in flight high in the
air, not against a mast.) Nevertheless, Jones's highly developed concept
of, indeed faith in, the human world as a diversity held in a unity of
sacred signs, of cultures and figures compounding myths, legends and
history into traditions which make sense *sub specie aeternitas*, can lead
him to either oversimplification or unreasonable confusion or both.
Certainly this seems to have happened in his coming to terms with *The
Rime of the Ancient Mariner*, which carries its own author's compound
of psychological, philosophical, religious and other approaches to human
experience.

Even putting aside Jones's lifelong obsession with ships and voyages,
one can see why he was attracted to Coleridge's poem. For, although it
has a straightforward linear structure, it has an extraordinary mix of
ingredients, mythical and historical, pagan to Christian. Think only of its
polar spirits, angels and Christian ghosts (which Jones discusses in his
'Introduction' but entirely omits from his illustrations – unlike his grand,
daring but would-be literal predecessor, Doré). It presents a Christian
land structure with kirk, hermit, priested wedding, Vespers – a godly,
ordered, social world; but, out on the open, lonely unexplored sea, when
the Mariner bites his arm and sucks the blood to call for help for himself
and a dying, parched ship's crew, along comes a spectre, a skeleton-ship
carrying Life-in-Death and Death dicing for their Fate: all Christian
notions of Providence are gone in a primitive notion of arbitrary fortune.
Moreover, reason or potential reason is thwarted by superstition, such as

about curses. (For Coleridge too, the Mariner with his oaths to saints and 'Mary Queen' is a superstitious pre-Reformation Christian.) The story also involves some arbitrary leaps in space and time (which, calculating the ship's impossible movements across the globe, Jones discusses with some pedantry); that is, the Mariner's experience has characteristics of dreaming.[6]

The Ancient Mariner (not in 1798, but in 1800, 1802 and 1805) was subtitled 'A Poet's Reverie' – a reverie being a waking dream, a dream with some conscious control in it. Scientists of Coleridge's time (such as Erasmus Darwin in *Zoonomia*, 1794) who characterized dreams, declared nightmare a form of reverie. But, without any prompting, the ordinary reader would agree that *The Ancient Mariner* describes a nightmare experience for the Mariner himself. Through the Mariner's tale, the Wedding Guest, kept away from the happy social event, the wedding, certainly goes through a nightmare; and we are told at the end that he woke up a changed man: 'A sadder and a wiser man / He rose the morrow morn.' (Jones disapproved of the 'sadder' as a Romantic superfluity (*DG*, 224).) If the poem is the poet's nightmare, then it includes the experience of the Mariner and the Wedding Guest – and perhaps the narrator too. All this is given as a nightmare experience to whomever reads it with sufficient self-projective sympathy. Jones himself declares that the tale 'spellbinds', that 'you and I' 'cannot choose but hear' (*DG*, 190).

There is plenty of contemporary, external commentary to inform us about Coleridge's inclinations as he wrote the poem. Some points to its dream ingredients. One inspiration was a dream by his friend Cruikshank about a spectre ship. De Quincey says in his *Recollections of the Lake Poets* that, before writing *The Ancient Mariner*, Coleridge had meditated a poem on 'delirium, confounding its own dream scenery with external things and connected with the imagery of high latitudes'. But, even in ignorance of examples such as these, the persistent references to dream in the poem provide signals for one's reading.

Other help towards our understanding is given in Coleridge's published explanation with his incomplete prose-poem 'The Wanderings of Cain' that the *Mariner* was written when a joint venture with Wordsworth to write about Cain failed. (Wordsworth could not write anything.) The weird 'Wanderings of Cain' seems to involve evil spirits masquerading as good, including the good Abel, together with some interchange of Cain and Abel – Abel becoming deathless – which should be Cain's state. Coleridge's association of the two works supports the seeing of the Mariner in terms of Cain and the Wandering Jew. He shoots the albatross, he pays an appalling penance at sea and remains a wanderer, a shape of terror, defined to himself by his own story, compelled to tell it to whichever unfortunates, like the Wedding Guest, get in his way. The Cain association directs us to the curse on the Mariner. The two hundred dying sailors curse him:

> Each turned his face with a ghastly pang,
> And cursed me with his eye. (III, 215–16)

If this recalls any curse in literature, it must be Adam's imagining all future generations cursing him for his original sin, in Milton's *Paradise Lost* (Book X, 733–5).

Otherwise, from Coleridge we have only his late comment on the poem when Mrs Barbauld complained that the poem carried insufficient moral (*Table Talk*, May 1830). Coleridge replied that the poem had too much moral. 'Madam', said Coleridge, 'the poem has the fault of obtruding moral sentiment as a principle or cause of action in a work of such pure imagination.' It ought, he said, to have had no more moral than that story in *The Arabian Nights Tales* in which a man throws a date stone over his shoulder and hits a genie which rises up and says it must kill him. Here, in this parallel, we have an amoral story with accidental, unreasonably connected events, a sin committed in ignorance with disproportionately dreadful results. But in his retort to Mrs Barbauld, is Coleridge dismissing that moralizing jingle at the end of the poem requiring that we should be kind to our fellow creatures? Certainly that moral seems an inadequate explanation of the terrible punishment of the Mariner which has gone before it and will never leave him.

Faced with just the story, one might well ask whether the Mariner should have suffered so much for shooting an albatross. That would be an irrelevant question, however, if the poem is read as a work of 'pure imagination'. In writing *The Ancient Mariner*, Coleridge may be exploring the question to what extent entry into the purely imaginary world is justified. He may be asking: if we move into a world of dreams, even reverie, of 'mental space',[7] with time and space contracted or expanded, with will, judgement, surprise suspended, with heightened senses and sensations, extraordinarily vivid scenery, *but* with no rational control of, or belief in, an overall rationally explicable order (such as is the experience of the Mariner on his 'silent sea') – what then?

My summary of Coleridge's *Ancient Mariner* begins to indicate what Jones chose to ignore of its 'riches' in his engravings and even in his

'Introduction'. He tones down the nightmare. (As a small pointer, where for Jones are the rescuing pilot, who falls down in a fit, and the pilot's boy of the poem, who, at least, indicate the terrifying effect of the Mariner: 'The Devil knows how to row' (VII, 569)?) Jones is fascinated by 'Life-in-Death' (spending ink in the 'Introduction' on considering her development from several traditions, including 'the chooser of the slain' (*DG*, 198–202)), but he does not seem to notice her real incompatibility with other elements of the story such as lead him to observe in an aside that the shooting of the albatross is 'not unsymbolic of the *Felix Culpa*' (*DG*, 197). He finds the 'Hermit good', asked to 'shrieve' the Mariner, an error in the poem, a 'stage-property', superfluous to its concept of perpetual penance (*DG*, 212–14); but again he softens what is fearful in the poem. The concept of friction and 'eternal partition' between a 'bad' Cain and a 'good' Abel appears in Jones's own poetry (such as *In Parenthesis*, 162), but Cain's as a parallel story does not figure for him apparently in his reading of *The Mariner*. In his engravings he devotes a full page to the advent of the 'spectre-bark' and its fateful crew, but he forgets entirely the natural and powerful spirits of vengeance which are equally real (or equally an illusion) in the Mariner's voyage; they do not fit into his scheme. One could say that as an anthropocentric writer, Jones's concentration is on the ship as part of Coleridge's imagery (which he sees conveniently as of 'metamorphic quality'), rather than on the sea. For Jones a ship is an 'argosy', the commercial vessel of man's life, preferably built in the shape of the church. But, in order to find this meaning in *The Ancient Mariner*, he ignores the fact that Coleridge's ship is ruined, its planks warped, its sails like brown skeletons of leaves, and that, like the unfortunate albatross before it, it sinks 'like lead' into the sea (IV, 291; VII, 549).

In some sense perhaps David Jones has recognized Coleridge's explorative voyage into a world of 'pure imagination' (the Mariner's sea), and has provided a safety-net himself in a selective rendering and interpretation of it, with flashes throughout and a resolution which signal that the Christian answer is always present in hints and signs within the direst experience and least expected situations. The result of this protective measure seems to be that it restricts his conveying the full value of a complex work, such as was his wish; moreover, his simplication (if in fact we accept his interpretation) may offer confusion where there is clarity.

> It is evident that this great poem, taken as a whole and in spite of various very differing themes ... cannot avoid evoking the Redeemer, our Odysseus, who in Homer, is, at his own command, made fast to the stepped mast. (*DG*, 214)

Christianity develops some spiritually useful textual and figurative paradoxes ('He that loseth his life . . . shall find it' (Matt. 10: 39)); it finds some analogies between stories of the Old and New Testaments; but it does not provide conflations or bindings of opposites of a kind such as where Cain prefigures Christ, 'The Redeemer'.

Wordsworth declared that for Coleridge 'The unity of all hath been revealed' (*The Prelude* (1850), II, 221). Jones, despite his high seriousness in attempting both in engravings and in words to find a unity with Coleridge's achievement, through his own creative strengths builds for himself considerable diversity

Notes

[1] My line references in this paper are to the text of *The Rime of the Ancient Mariner* of 1834 used in E. H. Coleridge (ed.), *The Complete Poetical Works of Samuel Taylor Coleridge*, 2 vols. (Oxford: Clarendon Press, 1912, repr. 1952, 1962), vol. I. There are indications that David Jones used such a fully annotated version; certainly he used a copy with Coleridge's late prose glosses of 1817.

[2] My page references to 'An Introduction' are not to the separate publication of it (1972) but to the text in *The Dying Gaul* (1978).

[3] I am indebted to Paul Hills of the University of Warwick for showing me Jones's drawings for the plates. My opinion is that the unifying 'undertone' in the engraved prints does not improve the drawings. Other critics may be more appreciative of Jones's technical achievement via the simple lines of copper-engraving. For example, Paul Hills notices Jones's use not of unwiped plates but of short hatchings within line contours for realistic effects:

> In the second plate, 'The Albatross', these hatched shadows do not insist upon the substantiality of bodies, but floating over the surface, describe the wind and space of the sea . . . Jones employed the abstraction inherent in the simplicity of line to disclose deeps and strata of meaning, a world of signs. (Paul Hills, *David Jones*, London: Tate Gallery, 1981, p.46)

It is a subtle difference between the drawing and the engraving which will incline one to appreciate the latter. The engraving 'The Albatross' contains very much more hatching than the drawing, and so conveys the movement of air and water disturbingly.

[4] Quotation from a private letter (1961), in J. Miles and D. Shiel, *David Jones: The Maker Unmade* (Bridgend: Seren, 1995), p.71.

[5] Jacques Maritain, *The Philosophy of Art*, tr. Fr John O'Connor (Ditchling: St Dominic's Press, 1923), p.22.

[6] The compression of time and space in the poem is only one of many dream ingredients incorporated into the poem. As Jones ignores the poem's dream character and its many references to dream, including 'the *Nightmare* Life-in-Death', I do not pursue these here. However, they do reinforce my view that the *Ancient Mariner* does not produce a Christian message in a major way.

[7] 'Mental space': I refer to these words in Coleridge's remarks on Spenser's *The Faerie Queene* which, he says, is made of 'a wondrous series of images, as in our dreams', being the 'land of Faery, that is, of mental space': 'The poet has placed you in a dream and you neither wish nor have the power to enquire where you are or how you got there' (T. M. Raysor (ed.), *Miscellaneous Criticism*, London: Constable, 1936, p.35).

To Make a Shape in Words:
The Labyrinthine Text of David Jones

TOM GOLDPAUGH

In the Preface to *The Anathemata* David Jones mentioned 'experiments made from time to time between 1938 and 1945' (*A*, 15). Parts of these early experiments were used in *The Anathemata* and others were later published as individual poems in *The Sleeping Lord and Other Fragments*. Of those 'experiments' Jones wrote, 'what was then written is another book' (*A*, 14).

In fact, these form what can be considered two other books. The original 'longer work begun c.1940' (*SL*, 3), alluded to in *The Sleeping Lord*, exists as a seventy-seven-page narrative set in Jerusalem on Holy Thursday; its speakers are Roman soldiers of occupation. Written between 1940 and 1943, it is the work from which Jones later extracted the Roman poems in *The Sleeping Lord*.[1] In addition, there is also a 143-page poem written between 1943 and 1946, the second half of which René Hague and Harman Grisewood published as *The Roman Quarry*. This second work evolved out of the earlier narrative to become *The Anathemata*'s immediate predecessor, a work Jones also called *The Anathemata*.

While important to understanding Jones's development, these two works are equally valuable as works in their own right. Begun at the opening of the Second World War, the narrative's condemnation of military and economic imperialism and its advocacy of local culture and regional diversity are central to Jones's cultural theories. The second work, written in three stages between 1943 and 1946, charts Jones's artistic growth from *In Parenthesis* to *The Anathemata*. Here he developed the linguistic and structural techniques that mark *The Anathemata* as he first attempted to build 'a heap of all that [he] could find' (*A*, 9), a text that was a verbal labyrinth that would protect what he felt were the endangered cultural signs.

Underlying Jones's work is his belief that the modern world is dying in the grip of industrialism and a developing world order that destroys the sacramental in the name of utility and economics. A letter he wrote to the *Catholic Herald* in the early 1940s is typical of his position: 'The main characteristics of our age and its products are obvious to all: the standardisation, the mass-production, the particular kind of organisation etc. – the characteristics of the mechanised "world-state".'[2] Even before he had published *In Parenthesis*, he had undertaken a work that addressed these concerns: 'The Book of Balaam's Ass'. From its inception, though, he called it a 'rambling affair ... about "ideas", the one thing I have always disliked in poetry' (*DGC*, 86). The only thing that gave it a shape, he wrote, was 'the continuity of my own rambling mind' (*DGC*, 91).

Although he finally abandoned the work, he did not abandon all of it. In March 1940 in a letter to Harman Grisewood he mentions a 'conversation at the time of the Passion' (*RQ*, 235). This 'conversation' developed into the narrative poem. What allowed him to move from the abandoned work to that conversation between two Roman soldiers on the walls of Jerusalem was his reading of Tacitus' *Annals of Imperial Rome* and his re-immersion in Spengler's *The Decline of the West*. Tacitus suggested parallels between Rome's Germanic wars and the world wars of the contemporary West, and his treatment of Rome's Teutoburg Forest campaigns spoke to Jones's own experiences in the First World War. Jones's rereading of Spengler provided an organizing principle for his analysis of civilization and culture. Offering a terminology and a system, Spengler's theories are to Jones's narrative what Vico's are to Joyce's *Finnegans Wake*.

Briefly, Spengler outlines how a living culture reifies into a sterile civilization as it moves through four stages from cultural spring to civilization winter. Spengler also proposes a morphological system where different time periods are contemporaneous on the same birth-to-death continuum. Imperial Rome with its expansionist wars and world economy, was a late-autumn civilization analogous to the twentieth-century West. In its imperialist stage, civilization first dominates and then assimilates local cultures to the megalopolis, a term coined by Spengler's English translator for *gross-städtisch*.[3] Pitting culture against civilization, Spengler provided Jones with a poetically useful geography for his own terms of opposition. It was under the auspices of Tacitus and Spengler, then, that Jones shaped his 'conversation at the time of the Passion' between two Roman soldiers of occupation.

The poem opens with a Catholic Mass in the present, and the first six sheets are very close to *The Anathemata*'s opening. In both, the Mass moves back to the Last Supper with almost identical lines:

> where a few
> are who gather in high room
> battened and one gone out.
> There's conspiracy here and birthday. (6/Folio 7A.1/*A*, 51)[4]

But where *The Anathemata* goes to the prehistory of 'Rite and Fore-Time', the narrative stays in the upper room at the moment the Eucharist is instituted until a bugle call echoes in from outside.

Here the narrative of two soldiers on guard duty on the walls of Jerusalem starts. The poem has two major parts and a number of submovements within each. The same complex spatial structures Thomas Dilworth noticed in the Roman poems are evident in the original.[5] The first part moves through the middle watch concurrent with Gethsemane and follows Crixus, a veteran of the German campaigns, and Oenomaus, a six-year veteran, as they look out over Jerusalem and reflect on the universal lot of soldiers of occupation. Ending with the invocation of the Great Mother later published as 'The Tutelar of the Place', the first part also includes 'The Wall' and 'The Dream of Private Clitus'. The second part moves from the end of the middle watch until dawn on Good Friday. Dominated by the same Brasso Olenius, first mentioned in 'The Dream of Private Clitus', it contains 'The Fatigue' and ends with 'The Tribune's Visitation'.

The narrative opens with the lines 'On night-gust, for the night relief, at / the night-wall' as a bugle sounds and

> cuts
> quadripartite the shadow-hours, disciplines
> the slack durations into columns of time. (7/Folio 23A 1)

Coming on guard for the middle vigil are Oenomaus and Crixus. Exploring the effects of economic and military imperialism on those who maintain the empire, this section underscores Jones's contempt for expeditionary wars and for the merchant classes who stay 'secure behind the wall / to drink the wine to break the bread', while Oenomaus, like all soldiers of occupation, 'is a stone in the living wall that circuits the city' (13), the 'urbs throughout the orbis' of imperialism. The speaker envisages a retired soldier in Rome holding out 'the cadger's palm for the small / change' who has left 'his nerves on the Frisian wire' (12–13), a line that evokes both the First World War and the Roman defeat at the Teutoburg Forest which the speaker has already called 'an extra nasty packet' (11).

Crixus speaks at the point, and the fragment published as 'The Wall' opens. Spengler's influence is explicit as Crixus asks if Rome was founded so that 'we should / sprawl from Septimontium a megalopolis that wills death' (20/*SL*, 13). Where 'The Wall' concludes with the lines

> we shall continue to march
> round and round the cornucopia:
> that's the new fatigue (*SL*, 14)

the narrative continues with the lines

> And you and I comrade, the Darlings of Irene,
> we shall continue to march, in convoy, to
> safeguard the distribution (24)

as Oenomaus and Crixus go on to discuss Tiberius at Capri.

With this, Oenomaus tells his mate that a change is about to take place in the world and 'they'll be needing / to reshuffle the formulas pretty soon' (24). In this movement Oenomaus and Crixus relate two very different dreams.

Oenomaus, seeing the Passover rituals, tells Crixus what 'the Sibyl of the wall would say' (24), and the work moves from a conversation between two soldiers into prophecy as Oenomaus foretells western history that will stem from this moment. This is an apocalyptic moment for Rome, the moment when 'the points of magnetism shift'. Something seems to be in the air:

> Times turn – the vatic times and times and
> half-times begin to be accomplished
> The years numbered from the foundation of the
> wall draw out – a new arithmetic
> measures the duration, from the transit of
> a new start they calculate a new day. (25)

Crixus acts as a fair critic when he responds, 'it was a bit on the long side, a bit flowery for my / liking, couldn't get the hang of much of it' (26).

This begins Crixus' reply, but where Oenomaus looks forward, Crixus recalls the past. Crixus also 'dream[s] of deliverers / ... on / the traverse of the wall, but I dream I'm m'own deliverer' (26), leading into 'The Dream of Private Clitus'. As in the published version, the original goes through three stages: the nightmare of Germans as large as trees; the shift to Rome's Ara Pacis where Crixus and his now-dead comrade are taken up by the statue of the Tellus Mater; and the dream of Crixus' childhood farm.

The original and the published versions are almost identical, save for linguistic embellishment and the later introduction of Celtic material. When Crixus mentions Brasso Olenius as

> part of the fabric, he is, he's on the
> permanent establishment, if ever a bastard
> was. (36)

Oenomaus asks if it is 'Brasso Olenius, the reg'mental'. Crixus replies 'he was up there with us, he's always been with us' (36/*SL*, 21), leading to an attack on 'the men / Of Empire, the men of prey who've made their pact with actuality' (37) without whom empire could not exist. The men of fact,

>   ... they're the
> bastards who gain immortality, Oenomaus,
> a solid, enduring, immortality of inheritance
> an immortality you can clap eyes on,
> and fingers, like you finger y'r donation
> when they shell it out. (37)

Empire's great crime, Crixus says, is that it destroys cultures and uproots people from place:

>   That's the cost
> of Empire, Oenomaus, that is. You can't stretch
> the navel string indefinitely and empire is
> a great stretcher of navel strings and a snapper
> of 'em, a great uprooter is empire – it's
> a great robber is empire, it robs the
> pieties, you can't have pieties to my way
> of thinking, unless you're rooted. (46)

Crixus then remarks on empire's spiritual counterpart – monotheism – which would deny

> a man's spirit a local
> habitation and in the name of brotherhood would
> orphan all the world and make the Great
> Mother weep,
> She who loves place, time, demarcation. (47A–48)

At this point 'The Tutelar of the Place', as originally spoken by Crixus, begins. This is the spatial centre of the narrative, occupying the same place in this work that Dai Greatcoat's speech holds in *In Parenthesis*. 'The Tutelar' also indicated Jones's objections to Spengler. In a letter of 26 February 1942, he pointed out his difficulty with Spengler:

> I've been immersed in Spengler, I'm battling with him, I've not measured him up yet! . . . He's so *right*, and, as I think, also *so wrong*. But I really can't tell quite where, or what, it is. I believe it resides in the Jackson Knight thing – he has liquidated *Juno*. It is a male thought-world entirely. (*DGC*, 115)

The Tutelar is Jones's alternative to Spengler's 'male thought-world'; 'the Jackson Knight thing' refers to Jackson Knight's *The Cumaean Gates*, which Jones said 'had a profound influence on me' (*DGC*, 213). In time, Jackson Knight's study of the labyrinth would supplant Spengler's morphology as the chief structural influence on Jones.

In *The Cumaean Gates*, Jackson Knight described maze dances as 'belonging to the larger class of protective rituals, performed to exclude evil influences',[6] and 'the movements of the perfomers are intended to weave a magical entanglement and spread a field of magical force to exclude all that is not wanted to enter the guarded place' (202). 'The Tutelar of the Place' is Crixus' equivalent of a maze dance, and dance imagery dominates the section:

> Sweet Mair devise a mazy-guard
> in and out and round about
> double dance defences
> countermuse and echelon meanders round the
> holy mound
> fence within the fence the wood within the wood
> pile the dun ash for the bright seed. (54/*SL*, 64)

Crixus invokes the Great Mother to 'save us . . . From the guile of the negotiators' who would 'square the world-floor' (53/*SL*, 62) by 'set[ting] up the hedges of illusion round some remnant of us' in 'the December of our culture' (54/*SL*, 64).

At its conclusion Crixus again reflects on imperialism and mono-theism, which leads into a discussion of one of the local messiahs:

> They say he cuts signs in his skin
> They say he makes signs on the ground
> They say he sees signs in heaven
>
> They say he is himself both sign and
> thing signified.

> They say he can raise a gale o' wind and
> still one.
> They say no tree can hang him but a cabbage tree. (57–8)

At this moment, the bugle sounds, the middle watch ends, and the second part of the work begins.[7] Crixus criticizes the Celtic trumpeter, leading him to ruminate on the Celts as a culture of mist, water and dreams, opposed to the 'ordered light . . . the clear sky where Caesar reigns' (60). He also outlines the economic penetration that prepares for the military:

> Once your Briton sees his drooped
> moustaches in a Corinthian mirror, sold
> him by a Greek Massiliot, off they'll
> come . . .
> What's freedom, what's autarchy, compared
> with smooth Sidonian glass. (63)

After this, Crixus and Oenomaus part company so as not to be caught speaking together (65).

Brasso enters, and the changing of the guard takes place with the lines 'relief Details – halt – fall out first file / for this post re-mainder order arms' (67/*SL*, 28). On questioning the two men, Brasso finds they have noticed a disturbance by the Water Gate which they could only see were they not at their respective posts, and he details them to a fatigue. The disturbance is Christ's arrest; the detail is his crucifixion.

Here a far shorter original version of 'The Fatigue' begins. Opening with the changing of the guard and the detailing of Crixus and Oenomaus, it moves to a short passage on how to avoid the more onerous jobs of an execution (68/*SL*, 33), and ends with a depiction of how one is assigned duties 'by regimental disposition by allocation . . . by your place on a corporal's order' (68/*SL*, 38). The middle watch is then dismissed to barracks and the narrative proceeds.

While the published version includes two later insertions, both were substantially completed before 1946. While making the final insertion into 'The Fatigue', 'the hundred or so lines [of] reflection made in the context of the Catholic Xtian tradition' (*SL*, 26), Jones first considered calling the work *The Anathemata* or *The Anathema* (125A).[8]

After the middle watch is dismissed, 'The Tribune's Visitation', spoken by Brasso begins. In this earliest version the setting moves to the guard house and begins with the admonition to the men to polish their brass. From there it moves directly to the beginning of the monologue with the lines 'Is this a hut on Apennine' (70) and, until the end, follows the published version, save for some minor changes in language.

In his speech to the men, Brasso takes the themes of the night and represents them from the standpoint of empire, although as a spokesman who is painfully aware of what has been lost. Brasso's response rounds out the earlier stock figure Crixus painted, making the loss of culture even more poignant, articulated as it is by one who sees the deprivation for what it is but who attempts to compensate through a community of loss under the imperial aegis.

The speech takes on even greater resonance than the published version when seen in the context of the whole narrative. When he claims that those who uphold the values of culture and the Great Mother are fools and that 'such bumpkin anathemas are for the / young time, for the dream watches – now we serve contemporary fact' (70/*SL*, 50), Brasso's words counter Crixus' prayer to the Great Mother. Jones's use of 'anathema' in the original version of Brasso's speech, later changed to 'sacrament' (*SL*, 50), is interesting. Its only other use is in 'The Tutelar of the Place' where the anathemas of culture – childhood, dreams, the maternal – oppose those of imperialism, as presented by Brasso.

Possibly the most disturbing of Brasso's reversals occurs when he unconsciously evokes the Last Supper. The narrative opens in the upper room with the institution of the Eucharist:

> the new code
> is promulgated in the oral style, he
> would have only intimate ears hear.
> The wary Didymus tries the shutter
> if it be firm, (he says) against the
> wolf-wind from the Potter's flats, if it
> be firm, (he thinks), against the eye
> without, against the hooded eye against
> the chink, the eye that guides the hand
> that jots the dossier –. (6/Folio 7a.1)

Now, in an upper room surrounded by his disciplines, Brasso creates the same condition:

> but set the doors to – let's stand
> within and altogether – let's shut out
> the prying dawn; the dawn-wind
> carries far and I have things to say
> not for the world-wind to bear away
> but for your ears alone to hear (76/*SL*, 57)

after which he institutes a sacrament of empire that counters the earlier institution of the Eucharist.

> See! – I break this barrack bread
> I drink with you this issue cup
> I salute with you these mutilated
> signa – I, with you, have cried
> with all of us the ratifying formula,
> Idem in me . . .
> if then, we are dead to nature,
> yet,
> we live to Caesar
> from Caesar's womb we issue
> by a second birth. (77/*SL*, 58)

Here the original narrative ends.

Everything about the narrative points to a highly crafted, complex and completed work. Jones, though, never published the poem. Even more problematic, the work does not explain how Jones artistically moved from *In Parenthesis* to *The Anathemata*. The narrative, in fact, is structurally identical to *In Parenthesis*.

In order to explore both issues, we need to look at *The Roman Quarry*. Containing bits and pieces of the Roman poems mixed in with Celtic poems and passages that suggest *The Anathemata*, *The Roman Quarry* clearly presents problems to a reader as it wanders from Jerusalem to Wales and back again. According to John Peck, it is 'an unworkable whole, whose disaster Jones's editors do not address . . . an art stuck in the prime matter of the cultural matrix'.[9] Regardless of whether one agrees with Peck's assessment, the text Hague and Grisewood published as *The Roman Quarry* is substantially the work that Jones called MS C, the second half of a 143-page poem.

In a memorandum dated 5 January 1980, Hague mentions a stray manuscript sheet that reads:

> Commence on p.3 of Manuscript B
> 'we already' etc. to 'doubts if they be sufficient' on P.7 of MS. B
> Inserted from pp.3 & 4 & 5 (?) & 16 & 17 of Manuscript A
> 'You can hear a penny drop' 'this one fetches more light' to bottom of p.6 MS. A
> Continue with p.7 MS. B
> 'On night gust etc'. to p.57 MS. B
> pp.58–143 MS. C intact
> From p.7 MS. A 'Soon will be the fracture of Branch' to end of MS. A
> (*RQ*, 283)[10]

Concluding that 'David must have muddled or changed the letters' (*RQ*, 282) and that MS A is 'The Old Quarry', MS B is 'The Roman Quarry' and MS C is 'The Judas Sequence', Hague constructed *The Roman Quarry and Other Sequences*. But Jones did not muddle the order. What Hague had found was actually the blueprint for the original version of *The Anathemata*.[11]

Despite present difficulties in reading *The Roman Quarry*, the work is far more unified than is first apparent. In fact, Vincent Sherry has recognized that the work has 'a strong internal coherence' and Peck's description of the work as 'a gigantic disinterment' (Peck, 369) is suggestive of the actual structure.

On 6 May 1943, Jones wrote to Tom Burns:

> I've been reading some elementary geology books lately . . . in the course of the thing I'm trying to write I had occasion to speak of a Roman road in Wales & a river which cuts it . . . I could not proceed without knowing what precisely the strata of those parts were made of . . . what the ground was like . . . and what the subsoil was like . . . and so on. (Group Purchase B/I/16)

This is the first mention of 'The Roman Quarry'. Begun in the spring of 1943, *The Roman Quarry* is Jones's attempt to embed a multi-levelled verbal labyrinth beneath the surface of an already existing narrative as a means of preserving the cultural deposits. It also marks the start of Jones's formal and theoretical shift to *The Anathemata*, as spatial structure supplanted temporal sequence and Jackson Knight displaced Oswald Spengler.

In the narrative, a Celtic recruit sounds the bugle announcing the change of guard leading Crixus into a meditation on how 'susceptible Britannia' will fall to Roman imperialism. Over manuscript pages 65, 66 and 67, he envisages the ships off the British coast, imagines the soldiers disembarking, recalls some Celtic deities he has heard of, and then evokes the image of the ship again. In the original version, Crixus ends by saying:

> So mate, their very signa we bring
> to them – let history weave but
> long enough.
> When Calibans of Logia Sinus swear by
> Bran that tree tops walk the spume
> because the green troughs hide all but
> the top trees of our cruising biremes. (*RQ*, 11 and 39/66)

Beginning with a meditation on Roman road building, Jones introduced forty-five manuscript pages of material in between the lines 'let history weave but long enough' and 'When Calibans of Logia Sinus swear by / Bran that tree tops walk the spume'. These forty-five pages form the bulk of *The Roman Quarry*. These pages, embedded in the narrative of the Roman soldiers on the walls, were introduced in three stages. With each stage, the poem moved further from the Roman 'surface', delved more deeply into Celtic deposits, and became more allusive and meditative. As the work moved further from the narrative, a new structural pattern emerged based in part on Jones's reading of Jackson Knight.

The first insertion, fifteen pages long, and marked 66A to 66N, predicts the Roman invasion of Britain. After describing the Roman ships off the Welsh coast, it moves to soldiers disembarking and follows the troops inland. Here Roman civilization, seen in the road and the bridge, confronts Celtic culture, seen in earth and water. When Roman roads and bridges cut into land, Jones introduces the Celtic deposits into the poem. The shift into the Celtic deposits occurs when an unnamed speaker asks,

> is the Afon Cych
> the Cocytus?
> Is Cothi of the quick-set hedge sad
> Acheron. (*RQ*, 14/66E)

Cocytus and Acheron are the last allusions to the classical world as the next five sheets descend into the geological and cultural deposits of Wales. Leaving Roman 'fact', we enter a world where 'hills like insubstantial vapours float' (*RQ*, 14/66F). Here

> race sleeps on dreaming race &
> under myth and overmyth
> like the leaf-layered forest floor are the uncertain crust. (*RQ*, 18/66G)

Entering the Celtic landscape we also leave narrative, and the text proceeds by interrogation and meditation. Finally we arrive at the megaliths and cairns that cover the land. In the question

> does the stone mastaba cairn the
> negotiator . . .
> does the holed-slab within the darkened
> passage keep the dark Promoter? (*RQ*, 19–20/66H)

we reach the centre of the fifteen-page insertion.

After this the text moves back up through the same geological deposits, along the roads and back to the coast where the ships wait. Just as we entered this Celtic world with allusions to the classical under-world, so also we leave it when we

> change our picquets at
> the Ivory Gate & trim the fast
> liburnae for service on the West Styx. (*RQ*, 39/66I)

At this point, we hear Crixus say, 'When Calibans of Logia Sinus swear by / Bran that tree tops walk the spume' (*RQ*, 40/66J). We are now back on the surface of the original narrative with Crixus and Oenomaus about to be put on fatigue the next day.

This insertion spirals downward into a spatial centre and then moves out again. The surface level – the watch on the walls – stops, and later restarts when Crixus mentions the Celtic horn playing. Inside of these two points, fifteen pages apart, are the opening and closing references to the coming conquest of the Celts by the Romans. Next are the parallel opening and closing images of the ships off the coast of Britain. When the poem moves into Celtic deposits, it does so with allusions to the underworld rivers of Cocytus and Acheron. When it moves out, it alludes to the Styx and the Ivory Gate. At the centre of the insertion is a stone cairn and a question. For the first part of the insertion, the movement is inward from the coast and downward through successive cultural layers. On reaching the stone burial chamber, the direction turns outward and upward and we pass the same markers going out as we met going in.

Jones completed the first insertion in the autumn of 1943, but it was only the first of three. Two later insertions followed the initial pattern: both were made between MS 66 and MS 67 of the original narrative, both were introduced at the centre of the previous one by splitting two lines, both moved inward and downward and then outward and upward.

Just as Spengler influenced the original narrative, Jackson Knight's study of labyrinths, *The Cumaean Gates*, influenced the form of the expansion.[13] Jones was fascinated by the labyrinth, and in the original narrative, the labyrinth is an important image. In what was finally published as 'The Wall', Crixus, an agent and victim of imperialism,

> walk[s] in darkness, in the shadow of the *onager*, in
> the shadow of the labyrinth of the wall, of the world.
> ... trapesing the macrocosmic night ...
> walking the inner labyrinth where also the night is. (*SL*, 14)

A 'stone in the living wall' (13), he is part of the very labyrinth that entraps him. This is imperialism's Daedalian prison, an image that occurs throughout the original narrative, most noticeably in what became 'The Fatigue', which traces the labyrinthine flow of power outward from its vacuous centre in Rome. From the 'wide-bevelled marble table' within 'the most interior-room', out past 'check-point Minotaur' and 'down through the departmental meander' (*SL*, 39), 'the ball slowly rolls' and 'your name and number on it', until it finally reaches the individual soldier who 'will furnish / that Fatigue' (*SL*, 41).

But there is another kind of labyrinth: the temenos, the protective labyrinth that encloses and protects the sacred object. 'The Tutelar of the Place', the original narrative's spatial centre, evokes such a temenos. In contrast to the 'robber walls of the world city' that form the Daedalian prison, the Great Mother is asked to 'set up hedges of illusion . . . twine the wattles of mist, white-web a Gwydion-hedge' (54/*SL*, 63) to confound 'the commissioners and assessors being the writs of the Ram'. The prayer, acting like a maze dance, verbally creates the sacred enclosure as 'ventricle and refuge both, asylum from the world storm' (*SL*, 64).

The original narrative employed the labyrinth in both roles: prison maze and protective temenos. The work's power derives, in part, from the tension between the temenos of culture that protects and the Daedalian world prison that entraps. Structurally, the two opposed labyrinths have their correlatives in the spatial centre of the hymn to the Great Mother and the temporal climax of Brasso's concluding speech.

Still, the earlier work only mimicked a labyrinth. What Jones set out to do with his insertions was to construct a work that would be a protective labyrinth, one that would literally enclose within it the endangered signa of the culture. A passage from 'The Old Quarry' outlines Jones's method and the direction of the project:

> You must be lost
> before you find the cornucopia
> at the core . . .
> at the navel
> of the spiral at Newgrange
>
> . . . It's always from
> chamber to chamber –
> in and out the creepway. (*RQ*, 182/96–7)

In the first insertion, the object at the centre is the burial chamber. Reading the first insertion and following its successively deeper layers is analogous to following the downward passage of the tomb. The first insertion asks who is buried in the 'stone mastaba' before returning to the surface. Jones's second insertion – a fourteen-page addition, labelled 66H1 to 66H14, explores this question.

This second addition continues the geological and cultural striation begun in the previous one and delves into the Celtic deposits. Out of this second insertion evolves both 'The Hunt' and the original version of 'The Sleeping Lord', Jones's hymn to the guardian of the land who is the land in which he is buried.

Beginning with an interrogation of the burial sites that cover the landscape, its direction is also downward into earlier cultural and geological deposits until the buried Sleeping Lord becomes the embodiment of the earth in a remarkable evocation of the land. This insertion, too, has a centre, and again it is a question:

> Does the land wait the sleeping lord
> or is the wasted land that very
> lord who sleeps (*SL*, 96/*RQ*, 37/66H12)

the lines that conclude the published version of 'The Sleeping Lord'. As soon as the question is asked, the text turns upwards again. Moving towards the Roman surface, classical allusions start to replace the Celtic: 'What was he called? Was his womb-name Cronus or had he another – Was he always the stern Maristuran' (*RQ*, 37/66H12). Soon we return to the surface 'at the brink of the lithosphere' of the Welsh landscape (*RQ*, 38/66H13). Here we come to the second half of the first insertion, the stone cairn we left fourteen pages earlier, and again we proceed back to the coast and to the Roman ships and finally to the surface of the text at MS 67, with Crixus on the walls.

Enclosed in the stone cairn of the first insertion, the second insertion recreates the land and the Sleeping Lord. Here the text-as-labyrinth becomes more pronounced, particularly through the textual embedding and the resulting shifts in point of view. In the first insertion, the invasion of Britain is embedded within the narrative simply as Crixus' comments on imperialism. The deeper interrogation of the stones is seen through the eyes of a Roman road-builder in a narrative within the narrative. In the second insertion, as 'The Hunt' leads directly into 'The Sleeping Lord', the text moves closer to a consciousness able to range through time.

From the original numbering of the pages, it is evident that Jones still considered the narrative of the Romans on the walls and the two Celtic insertions to be one work. The second insertion, though, altered the shape of the entire work. After Jones wrote what would finally evolve into 'The Sleeping Lord', the double-spiralled design of his verbal labyrinth became clearer. In effect, there were now two interrelated spatial 'centres'. Complementing the Great Mother who closes the first half of the text, a half Jones would later call MS B, is the mythic Sleeping Lord who opens the second half of that text, which he later labelled MS C. Together they form the male and female principles of culture that counter imperialist civilization's perversion of those principles, the Ram and the Ram's Wife.[14]

At this point, Jones added one last insertion which delved even more deeply into the past, his purpose now to recover and to enclose the cultural deposits and not simply to expand a narrative. The first insertion introduced the interrogative form that dominates *The Anathemata* while the second presented a consciousness capable of ranging through time. The third insertion offers the cross-temporal and cross-cultural linguistic allusiveness associated with *The Anathemata*. Continuing to the deepest deposits, the last insertion of fourteen pages – 66H12a to 66H12n – attempts to recover the thalassic tradition of the Island in all of its cultural changes. Presented as a quest for 'Manannan, deep of counsel', a Celtic sea god, this insertion attempts to include the full range of cultures that have left their mark on the region: Celtic, Norse, German, Latin, Christian and pre-Christian alike. Like the first and second insertions, the third continues the interrogative. Here, the questions ask 'where is he?' and 'who is he?'

Inserted between the lines

> does the Tawe clog in his grief?
> Do the troughing streams fill with his
> Chrism'd sweat (*SL*, 91/*RQ*, 28 and 36/66H11)

the final movement begins with the mingled tears and sweat of the Sleeping Lord who mourns for the wasted land. Here the tears become the rivers of Wales. Beginning with the Usk, the work names the Tawe, the Rhonddas, the Taff, the Rhymni and all of the rivers that flow through the southern coalfields of Wales to the Bristol Channel and the Severn. On reaching the ocean, the text moves to the coast of Ireland. Enquiring 'if he is to West' in Leinster or north 'leagued with the Gynt', the quest proceeds up the coast to 'where Dalriada whites to Kintyre' and 'off Larne' (*RQ*, 30/66H12c), finally reaching the Isle of Man, Manannan's centre of activities. It then turns back to the Welsh coast, beginning at the Wirral, moving across to Clwyd and Holywell, going around Anglesey towards the Llŷn peninsula, and returning back to its beginning at the Severn (*RQ*, 30/66H12g).

Such a rapid geographic survey does not account for the movement's intricacy. The section is like a whirlpool where cultures, beliefs and times are brought together. One passage illustrates that linguistic and cultural density:

> is he sud of the mull
> & thudding his Bradda, or
> lolled asleep
> not winking a limpid ripple
> from Bride to Maughold, to bluff
> the porphery silts on his nomen-isle
> or, with a long snook for Halycon
> quit by his south-port, showing his back
> to his Maug-holm
> his paddy up
> his grey coat on
> his phantom-dappled
> brume-white
> under the hurrying scud
> on Solstice-night
> Straight for the Wirral
>
> Wave is rough and
> Cold is wind
> but
> bright is *candela*
> God! he'll not douce with
> Deva-water their Plugain lights!
> Nor brackish her well for
> 'Frida Hygiea. (*RQ*, 30–1/66H12c)

Geographically, the lines move from Larne on the Ulster coast to the Isle of Man and on to the northern Welsh coast. Within that movement Jones linguistically compresses the pre-Christian Celtic, the Latin and the Christian. 'Mull' is Gaelic for a promontory while 'sud' is both the singular for 'suds' and an obsolete form for flood waters, meaning 'to foam'. Latin influence is felt in the word 'nomen'. 'Thudding' is most evocative, and describes Manannan's movement across the waters. A blast of wind, or a squall, it is also a clap of thunder, preparing for Manannan's identification with Wotan and Zeus as 'Father Thunderer / gone for a sailor' (*RQ*, 35/66H12h).

As Manannan moves 'Straight for the Wirral' the cultural compression takes on a different form. The location is Holywell where Christian and Roman are joined in the same 'Frida Hygiea'.

Here we find St Winifred, to whom the well was sacred, linked to Hygieia, a goddess of health and daughter of Aesculapius. The line 'bright is *candela*' alludes to rites of St Brigit, but, being of pre-Christian origin, she is a leading Celtic deity. Just as Manannan shares affinities with Wotan and Zeus, Brigit is analogous to Minerva and Athena. Even in the lines 'God! he'll not douce with / Deva-water their Plugain lights!' the Christian and pre-Christian are condensed. 'Plugain lights', a note tells us, were part of local Matins service, while Deva was the name of the local Roman garrison.

Returning down the coast, the speaker enquires 'Where's Nuada', a Celtic sea god and war god, equated with Nodens, a Celtic god of healing. Here the questioner asks:

> Where's the Roarer, or was he
> the Strider, or what, by his
> shape-shifting name, is he properly
> called?
>
> they're all shape-shifters – all a
> changeling bunch of amphibious hierarchs
> refracted in a misted prism. (*RQ*, 34/66H12g)

The effort to recover and reconcile all within the heritage continues as Celtic, Teutonic and Latin merge:

> Nuada he is
> of west waters
> a Wotan of deeps
> a wolf-meeter, a hand-loser . . .
>   denominate him once for all
> hand him a fish-spear, treble-barbed
> and call him Poseidon, but,
> remember
> he's half a Mars, if not Father Thunderer
> gone for a sailor. (*RQ*, 35/66H12h)

Here the text becomes a swirling cycle, the quest juxtaposing pre-Roman Celtic antiquity and Dark Ages Norse with Jones's memories of his childhood visits to north Wales. Celtic gods and goddesses, Roman and Germanic deities and Christian saints are all melded, 'shape-shifters . . . refracted in a misted prism' (*RQ*, 34/66H12g) that form the deposits. Structurally, this is the labyrinth's centre, at the same time that its interrogative rhetoric resists finality.

The third insertion brought to a close the series of Celtic insertions that Jones made into his original Roman narrative. Capable of standing on its own, the third insertion is a remarkable piece of writing where we first see the linguistic density and rhetorical style of *The Anathemata*.[15] Taken together, the three insertions begin the process that *The Anathemata* completes: to compress as much cultural resonance as possible into a passage through the medium of the individual word.

While Jackson Knight's study of the labyrinth influenced the formal development of the text and probably provided Jones with the initial impulse to create a verbal labyrinth, there was an equally important shift in Jones's theoretical orientation that reinforced the direction of his experiments. Throughout his career Jones was motivated by two very different theoretical views. One was the already mentioned cultural critique based on Spengler. The other was a sacramental theory grounded in the Eucharist. However, the two are, in some ways, incompatible. Although Spengler provided a machinery and structure for Jones's original narrative and allowed him to attack contemporary conditions, ultimately Jones disagreed with Spengler's assertion that cultural death was irreversible. In fact, the task of an artist, he claimed, was 'to carry forward into the present the traditions of the past and so make them available for the future' (Group Purchase C/1).

Jones's sacramental theory implicitly countered the pessimism of Spengler. To Jones, art was a subclass of sacrament and the artist's model was the Eucharist. His theory was based, in part, on his belief that the artist acted as 'rememberer' for a culture. One way in which a work of art functioned sacramentally was by including within it other cultural signs and 're-calling' them. The newly fashioned artefact spoke to the modern world and carried forward the past by embodying the deposits in a valid sign for the present. It was the literary equivalent of the doctrine of anamnesis.

Jones first outlined his concept of art as inclusive in 1935 when he wrote that 'the successful work of art is one where no ingredient of creation is lost, where no item on the list in the Benedicite Omnia Opera Dominum is denied or forgotten . . . [it is] incarnational.'[16] In a draft of a letter to Vernon Watkins he wrote:

> of a picture, a poem or what you will, we want to be able to say . . . something which the whole world cannot comprehend or hold has been enclosed within the strict confines of this or that . . . or any of the other 'carpentries of song'. (Group Purchase A/V/1).

In this sense, a work of art, particularly one which relies on the deposits for its material, is a temenos, a protective enclosure. Jones's verbal labyrinth formed from the Celtic deposits buried beneath the Spenglerian surface of the narrative was his attempt to 'carry forward into the present the traditions of the past' by making them available in a sign valid to the present.

There was, though, still the issue of form. Writing to Jim Ede in May 1943, Jones claimed that the problem in a work of art was to shape it so that it would achieve 'transubstantiation' whereby the work '*is* the scene or whatever it may be, stated in other terms' (L.47/1977, 13 May 1943). It was not enough for the theme of the labyrinth to be present in the work, as it had been in the earlier narrative. For his sign to be valid, for there to be an effectual recalling, the work had to be a temenos, a verbal labyrinth, made out of the very signs it sought to protect.

In this, *The Roman Quarry* is more perplexing than the original narrative. Jones clearly saw the work as a failure of form and felt that it never came together because he was unable to make the necessary connections. It can be argued that over the course of the insertions Jones developed the spatial structure and linguistic characteristics that mark *The Anathemata* as the verbal equivalents that allowed him to build such a temenos out of the signs of the culture.

The problem Jones faced with 'The Roman Quarry' was expressed, at least indirectly, by Hague:

> David was, to my mind, odd and mistaken in the importance he attached to typographic arrangement on the page. He took a good deal of pains over this, and I believe it was wasted on the reader, because printing has not the flexibility he needed. (*RQ*, 215)

Hague was right. Print did not offer Jones the flexibility needed to reproduce what he envisaged in *The Roman Quarry*. It was an attempt to create verbal depth perspective, to form the equivalent of the delicate layering of his paintings. But print, bound by flat text, could not offer perceptual depth.

The difficulty, finally, was not with his vision, so much as with the technical means available at the time. Walter Benjamin commented that 'the history of every art forms shows critical epochs in which a certain art form aspires to effects which could be fully obtained only with a changed technical standard, that is to say, in a new art form.'[17] *The Roman Quarry* clearly aspires to such effects. We have a highly experimental text that might, and I want to stress the provisional nature of this comment, find form in a new medium, hypertext, rather than traditional print. Considering Jones's antipathy to the modern world, there is some irony in this.

I would suggest that *The Roman Quarry* is more than a brilliant failure and more than a 'Rosetta stone for the poet's later writings', as Sherry has described it.[18] What we have in *The Roman Quarry* is a cohesive, even if incomplete work. What we have is a multi-levelled labyrinth created from the very deposits that we seek to preserve.

Notes

[1] For a fuller treatment of the seventy-seven-page narrative, see my article 'On the Traverse of the Wall: The Lost Long Poem of David Jones', *Journal of Modern Literature*, XIX (1995), 31–55.

[2] Group Purchase C/1; other manuscripts from this collection are similarly identified in parentheses. I wish to thank the Trustees of the Estate of David Jones and the National Library of Wales for permission to cite from the unpublished writings of David Jones.

[3] Oswald Spengler, *The Decline of the West*, tr. C. F. Atkinson (London: George Allen & Unwin Ltd, 1926).

[4] All pages of this manuscript and the subsequent one are in the National Library of Wales, Aberystwyth. The only sheets that have been catalogued are those that were part of the 1978 Purchase Group as identified drafts of *The Anathemata*. Where available, I have used Jones's numbering system and where applicable page numbers from *The Anathemata*, *The Sleeping Lord and Other Fragments*, and *The Roman Quarry and Other Sequences*.

[5] Thomas Dilworth, *The Shape of Meaning in the Poetry of David Jones* (Toronto: University of Toronto Press, 1988). Dilworth is the first critic to explore the intrinsically spatial structures of Jones's work, and my research is indebted to him.

[6] W. F. Jackson Knight, *Vergil: Epic and Anthropology*, ed. John Christie (London: George Allen & Unwin, 1967), p.199. All subsequent citations in parentheses.

[7] The first three lines are on MS sheet 57, the remainder on 58. It is here that René Hague begins *The Roman Quarry*. In starting *The Roman Quarry*, Hague cut the lines on 58 from the Roman Quarry sequence 'because I felt that these were a rather dauntingly theological opening' (*RQ*, 218). Sheet 58 was also numbered 1, although at a later stage of the project. Based on Jones's comment that he intended to begin his new work with a bugle call, Hague used the sheet numbered both 58 and 1 as the start of *The Roman Quarry*. In fact, it marked the start of the second half of the narrative. It seems that the actual opening bugle call on MS 7 was not in Hague's possession, having already been sent to the National Library of Wales with the *Anathemata* manuscript sheets.

[8] In a letter to Harman Grisewood on 4 July 1945, Jones comments that Jackson Knight 'thought *The Anathemata* was the accurate title for my thing in more ways than one' (*DGC*, 130). On the back of one of the insertion sheets Jones has 'The Anathema' and 'The Anathemata' carefully lettered.

[9] John Peck, 'Poems for Britain, Poems for Sons', in John Matthias (ed.), *David Jones: Man and Poet* (London: The National Poetry Foundation, 1988), p.368.

[10] What Jones called MS B was the first part of the original narrative, up to and including 'The Tutelar of the Place'. While MS A is more problematic, it appears to be the Judas sequence.

[11] Given the chaotic state of Jones's papers at the time of his death, his penchant

for ordering and reordering, and his numbering system that can best be described as labyrinthine, Hague's conclusions and subsequent ordering were logical. Clearly I am indebted to Hague and Grisewood, and my research is based upon their work.

[12] Vincent Sherry, '*The Roman Quarry* of David Jones: Extraordinary Perspectives', in Matthias, *David Jones*, p.394.

[13] While Jones's debts to Spengler, de la Taille and Maritain have been noted by critics, Jackson Knight's influence has been ignored. In the Preface to *The Anathemata* Jones cited Jackson Knight as second to Christopher Dawson. His comment is interesting and frames the influence in terms of labyrinths: 'Then there is Mr W. F. Jackson Knight whose particular *numen* or sprite is something of an Ariadne, who pays out more than one length of thread' (*A*, 36).

[14] Shortly after the second insertion Jones divided the entire text in half, probably for organizational purposes. The first fifty-seven pages – ending with the lines 'They say he is both / Sign and thing signified' – formed the MS B mentioned in the stray sheet Hague cites (*RQ*, 283). MS C consisted, at this point, of fifty-eight sheets: eighteen sheets form the original narrative, fifteen sheets form the first insertion, the three- and fourteen-sheet sequence of the second insertion, and eight sheets introduced at 'The Fatigue' and 'The Tribune's Visitation'. At this stage he started at what was originally MS 58 and renumbered it all, starting with 1 and proceeding to 58 (the two 58s are purely coincidental).

Jones's division of the text in half points up the double-spiralled nature of the whole work, with the Great Mother on one side and the Sleeping Lord on the other. In many ways, this simply strengthens the already existing mirroring of the first and second half, particularly the opposition between Christ and the Tribune.

That Jones considered it all part of one text is evident from the stray sheet to which Hague refers. That it was still growing is also obvious. The third major insertion of fourteen sheets – in addition to two other elaborations of seven and five sheets respectively at the 'The Fatigue' and 'The Tribune's Visitation' and two one-page transitions – brought the second half to eighty-six pages. All of these insertions pre-dated *The Anathemata*, and it was only after the creation of the 143-page manuscript that he considered calling the work *The Anathemata*.

[15] In fact, manuscript evidence very strongly suggests that 'Middle-Sea and Lear-Sea' evolved out of the third insertion section.

[16] Cited from the biography that Jones wrote for Jim Ede in 1935 (L47.1977/10, Kettle's Yard).

[17] Walter Benjamin, 'The Work of Art in the Age of Mechanical Reproduction', in *Illuminations: Essays and Reflections*, tr. Harry Zohn (New York: Schocken Books, 1969).

[18] Sherry, '*The Roman Quarry* of David Jones', p.393.

Time's Disc Jockey: Meditations on Some Lines in The Anathemata[*]

R. S. THOMAS

Waiting for the tale to begin,
not knowing that we are the tale,
that it began with us
and that with us it will end.
There was many a false start
but always the electrons were busy,
that dance in which to perish
was to survive in a different orbit.
We asked our questions and passed
on. The answer, discovered
by others, was to a different question.
Yet they, too, had the feeling
of having been here before.
We are our own ghosts, haunting
and haunted. We live out a dream,
unable to equate the face
with the owner, the voice
with the speaker, the singer
with the song. Ah, how we thought
science would deliver us, when
all it has done is to set us
circling a little more swiftly
about a self that is an echo.

This is not a cogent paper. It is not a tidy presentation of a theme. David Jones was a scholarly poet, and I am no scholar. Hence the title of my talk which allows me to ramble and also to conceal my lack of detailed knowledge of my subject. Nor is the title strictly correct, because I wish only to circle about the preface to *The Anathemata*, hoping that a few feeble sparks may fly to incinerate the richer tinder of your own minds. The words I have in mind are: 'It was a dark and stormy night, we sat by the calcined wall; it was said to the tale-teller, tell us a tale, and the tale ran thus: it was a dark and stormy night . . .'

I don't know whether Jones was quoting from a text I am ignorant of. It has been suggested to me that he himself is the author. They are memorable words. I find them fascinating. Some of that fascination comes from the word 'calcined'. I see shadows against a fire-lit wall; they are those of listeners to a *cyfarwydd* in a mediaeval Welsh hall. Jones was fascinated by the past, especially the Welsh past. My theme, however, is the idea of circularity suggested by the words and the interplay between fact and fiction. It begins with a statement of fact: 'It was a dark and stormy night, we sat by the calcined wall; it was said to the tale teller, tell us a tale, and the tale ran thus.' Clear and unequivocal. We asked for a story; but it began like this: 'It was a dark and stormy night'; a repetition of fact which at once becomes fiction. We are reminded of Borges's story of Pierre Ménard's rewriting of *Don Quixote*. He repeats it word for word, line by line. But what a difference, remarks Borges. He is recreating by the very fact of retelling. Consider also the repetition in Beckett's *Krapp's Last Tape*. Apart from trained actors, is it possible to repeat correctly, much less keep the overtones and nuances the same? You know that amusing game where a message is passed verbally to a person at the head of a row, and is then repeated in the ear of each successive member of the row. When the last person is asked to repeat out loud what he has received, the result is often farcically different. What is the difference between the photograph of a person and his portrait? Of a number of different studies, which is the real person? What is a person? Who am I? Who are you? A few years ago on sound radio there was a programme called *A Word in Edgeways* in which a panel of three or four speakers with a chairman discussed a certain subject. I suggested they consider the question of personality, which they did, not very successfully.

This discussion is about David Jones. The title suggested for me was 'Time's Disc Jockey', playing on the initials DJ. I am not quite sure what a Disc Jockey is, unless he is one who puts on many discs. Which ones did this DJ play? One of them was called *In Parenthesis*. What is life? Are art, love and society its main features, with war, money and the machine in parenthesis? Or are war, industry and money its main realities, with art and love in parenthesis? I don't associate much with scientists, technologists and the business world. Do they feel that theirs is the real world, and art and love merely things by the way? Is it only the humanities that tend to look before and after and pine for what is not? Is it only they who respond to such lines as: 'We are such stuff/As dreams are made on; and our little life/Is rounded with a sleep'?

A great distance separates the contemporary sophisticated world from that of the tale-tellers. The film, the theatre, the press, the novel, the media supply our need for a tale. But what do they give us really? Take the novel, one of the most popular time-passers. Fiction with its bleat that none of its characters bears any relation to any living persons. Do a novelist's characters remain always firmly under his control? Defoe's *Journal of the Plague Year* is now recognized as fiction, whereas his *True Relation of the Apparition of Mrs Veal*, once thought of as fiction, is now seen as an actual account of what Canterburians thought true. And what about Dickens's serialized novels, when crowds would gather to learn in advance what had happened to one of the characters in crisis? When I was in Manafon among the hard-bitten farmers, *The Archers* was already beginning its long run of popularity. Walter Gabriel, with his well-known rustic burr, was invited to open a neighbouring country fair. He disillusioned the villagers by turning up in a well-cut suit with what Dylan Thomas would have called a cut-glass accent. Have you been disturbed like me, by Marlow's repeated request to 'Pass the Bottle' in his part as narrator in Conrad's novel *Youth*? Or by other novelists pausing to exclaim, 'It was just like a novel'? Again I ask: What is life? Remember Plato's parable of the cave. We can be conditioned to accept so much. All that the fiction-makers ask of us is the willing suspension of our disbelief. Are we too gullible, ready to be conned? What about authors who pass off autobiography or biography as fiction, or fiction as autobiography? Or what of biography itself? How relate the many accounts of a person's life to his diaries, his photographs, his portraits?

Which brings me to history. Remember the quip that history was the lie which historians had agreed to tell. A whole series of lectures could be given on questionable texts. I never despise scholarship, the result of patient and admirable study of texts over scores of years, trying to decide the truth behind some scribe's account of what he thought, or had been told, had happened. You remember G. J. Williams's poem 'Gwladus Ddu'. R. G. Collingwood in his *The Idea of History* has many wise things to say about history and its writing. He rightly inveighs against a too positivistic treatment of it, based on a credulous belief in access to facts; yet his definition of the historian as one who re-enacts the past in his own mind, itself raises problems germane to this paper. If a historian is not only a spectator but a maker of history, how does he excel the novelist or the poet? Is Graves's novel about the Emperor Claudius inferior, or better than a historical account? Does not Jones in *In Parenthesis*, or Wilfred Owen in such poems as 'Exposure', give a more realistic account of trench warfare than the military historians? A weakness that has afflicted some historians such as Spengler and Toynbee and, among poets, Yeats and to some extent Eliot, is to see history as circular. The same elements, the same characters recur and must go on doing so in accordance with some mysterious but inexorable law.

'Man has his exits and his entrances.' It accords with an experience or a feeling which most of us partake of at one time or another. How many of us have not experienced on occasion a feeling of déjà vu? Suddenly, without warning, as we go about our daily business, there comes the conviction that all this has happened before. Is it a dream, or are we recalling? Owing to the millions of cells constituting a human brain, together with the electric circuits connecting them, maybe it is the events that have been recorded and forgotten which are recalled or by the psychoanalyst reactivated. Maybe it is just a personal trait, popular with us because it encourages fantasies: 'When I was a prince in Babylon and you were a Christian slave'. Or maybe it is because it bolsters our sense of solidarity with the species.

> Then, 'twas before my time, the Roman
> at yonder heaving hill would stare;
> the blood that warms an English yeoman,
> the thoughts that hurt him, they were there.

Or to emphasize our classical learning, we can identify with Eliot's lines:

> The nightingales are singing near
> the Convent of the Sacred Heart,
>
> and sang within the bloody wood
> when Agamemnon cried aloud . . .

I am subject to correction by the evolutionists, bearing in mind Darwin's finches, but generally speaking, one of the delights of bird-watching is to remark creatures that are repeating behavioural patterns which pre-date us by tens of millions of years. As has been said, nature knows no history. It is man who creates history. The fact that a nightingale sang in a wood a million years ago is not part of history. But the fact that it was heard 'in ages past by emperor and clown' gave birth to Keats's ode to it. As J. Hillis Miller has shown in his examination of Hardy's poem 'On Wessex Heights', that 'we are compelled to repeat not only patterns from our past lives, but also those more general patterns into which the universal experience of mankind has forced him' was an obsession with Hardy, as witness the well-known conclusion to *Tess of the d'Urbervilles*. Yeats, too, not only identified with past figures, both literary and actual:

> I am Timon and Lear or that William Blake
> that beat upon the wall
> till truth obeyed his call

but also made recurrence the theme of his powerful little play *Purgatory*:

> The souls in purgatory that come back
> to habitations and familiar spots relive
> their transgressions and that not once
> but many times.

Then in that strange book *A Vision*, he worked out an intricate system based on the great wheel that turns through a millennium, and of the gyres that spin upon themselves, forcing people to conform to certain repetitive or conflicting types, or to be torn between opposites according to the phases of the moon. And, as has been already mentioned, we have prose variants of this in such historians as Spengler and Toynbee. Or, as another variant on this theme of repetition, where the mother in Ibsen's *Ghosts*, hearing the laughter of her son as he sports with the housemaid, sees her own husband's folly being repeated all over again. It is a tragic or depressing feature of human life that, as Hillis Miller says apropos of Hardy, 'once something has happened it never ceases to exist, but repeats itself over and over.' Human history, as Hardy sees it, is a pattern of sameness emerging from difference, or as the French have it, *Plus ça change, plus c'est la même chose*.

How can we escape from this labyrinth? Or how can I escape from the one I have got myself into? There is another of Borges's parables about a prisoner whose captors so arrange things that he is shown a light at the end of a tunnel only to find that when he reaches it they are waiting for him, to demonstrate the refinements of cruelty by which an illusion or a dream can be punished.

Or consider how insistent children are upon the oft-heard story's being repeated word for word and in exactly the same word order. We, perhaps, can grow up in this respect, but cannot outgrow our desire for fiction, or for a funny story which we know to be less than half true. As Robert Penn Warren ends his long poem 'Audubon':

> Tell me a story.
>
> In this century and moment of mania,
> tell me a story.
>
> Make it a story of great distances and starlight.
> The name of the story will be Time.
> But you must pronounce its name.
>
> Tell me a story of deep delight.

There we go. As Eliot said: Mankind cannot bear too much reality. Or is it because reality is not enough, that we want it turned into a story, or sublimated in a poem? 'They were born, they suffered, they died.' Is that a true synopsis of human life? Or, as Eliot put it on another occasion: 'Birth, copulation and death. I'd be bored. You'd be bored.' What a drab thing fact is. 'Ah, que la vie est quotidienne!' So we demand fiction, praising most those who make fiction sound like fact. Is this what Stevens meant? 'Notes towards a Supreme Fiction'. Remember his 'Asides on the Oboe' which begins like this:

> The Prologues are over. It is a question now
> of final belief. So say that final belief
> must be in a fiction.

What is fiction? Fingo, fingere – to fashion, to form. In English it has come to mean what is not factual or true. Welsh has, as so often in its coinings, followed suit. 'Ffuglen' – false writing. Stevens said that one of the great human experiences was to see the gods disappear and die. And what was to fill the vacuum left by such? Our fictions? This is Matthew Arnold over again who claimed that as religion died, so poetry must take its place. I have referred to Stevens's long poem, 'Notes towards a Supreme Fiction', whose three sections are headed: 'It must be abstract', 'It must change', 'It must give pleasure'. Rather thin gruel for the soul, I should say. But as Stevens said elsewhere, 'the absence of the imagination had itself to be imagined.'

You remember Coleridge on the imagination. The nearest we can approach to God is as creative beings, and as creators we echo the creative act of the primary imagination. Jones was a religious man, as, I would contend, most creative artists of any substance are. He ended one of his fine poems, 'The Sleeping Lord', with a question most pertinent to this essay, which I will quote presently. Stevens, in his long poem, 'The Comedian as the Letter C', made two statements: firstly, 'Man is the intelligence of his soil'; then, 'His soil is man's intelligence. That's better. That's worth crossing seas to find.' It's the difference, I would say, between those who believe that mind has evolved from matter, and those who believe in the primary condition of mind, that esemplastic principle behind the universe. Like the Germans, we Welsh are excited by the word 'soil'. 'Mae pridd Cefnddwysarn arno.' But Wales was not always here. It is a product of the mind in contemplation, in its experience of the soil. 'The Sleeping Lord' ends with the question: 'Does the land wait the sleeping lord, or is the wasted land the very lord who sleeps?' Or in Stevens's terms, is this the sleep of death, the demise of the imagination; or is it a reference to the myth of Arthur, who is not really dead, but asleep in a cave somewhere in the hills, surrounded by his knights, awaiting the summons to arise and come forth and free his people from their chains?

We have considered the question of circularity, to which myth can be closely allied. One popular assessment of Christianity is that it appeared at a time when people were fettered by a belief in repetition, in the belief that life was an endless succession of rebirths, and that it offered them the promise of breaking free from such by introducing the concept of a historical end to the world at which the people of God would be resurrected into a changed existence. This is the springtime of the imagination. It offers hope. Is the fascination of circularity and fate a lassitude of the species? Is it a form of the death wish? Consider the enormous popularity of Fitzgerald's version of Omar Khayyam at the end of the nineteenth century.

> The Moving Finger writes; and, having writ,
> Moves on: nor all thy Piety nor Wit
>   Shall lure it back to cancel half a Line,
> Nor all thy Tears wash out a Word of it.

Was that *fin de siècle* malaise, and has our own taken a different form in which we believe that the only truth in life is that which can be repeated by experiment? What to do? Can we wring a truth out of what science tells us about the electron or is science's belief also a fiction? It tells us that as the electrons whirl about their nucleus at dizzying speeds, one will suddenly leap into a new orbit. Can we liken that to the resurrection with its promise of an new sphere for the purified soul? Much of Jones's work was a protest against the twentieth century's myth of an annual increase of 5 per cent in profits, a colonization of the stars and the freedom to acquire even more and more consumer goods at the expense of the earth's resources. Are we free to choose? The believers in circularity say, 'No'. Some scientists, certainly the geneticists, say 'No'. Christians, and all believers in the spirit must answer 'Yes'. 'For the Spirit and the bride say "Come". And let him that heareth say "Come". And let him that is athirst come; And whosoever will, let him take the water of life freely.'

Notes

*Delivered at a Conference on David Jones, University of Wales, Lampeter, September 1995.

Index